THE NEW AGES OF MEN

A practical guide for modern masculinity

Nick Clements

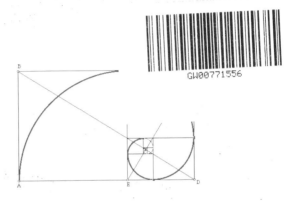

GW00771556

Sound of the heart

Comments and feedback on the book

'Gave me hope for my son, and suggested ways for me to support him.'
-   V. B.   Mother

'Made me think, it's funny as well as poignant."
-   E. N.   Vicar

'I want to buy this book for all my ex-boyfriends!'
-   R. F.   Journalist

'As a parent…this is a very useful book.'
-   D. S.   Father of two boys

'Helped me understand men and why they behave the way they do.'
-   M. M.   Healer and alternative therapist

'Inspires me to continue the work I am doing, many insights into working with men, really useful.'
-   G. C.   Social Sciences Student

'A more up-to-date Steve Biddulph, more practical and comprehensive.'
-   T. I.   Local authority community worker

Other titles by the author:

Pioneers Improving your School Environment

Murals, Mosaics, Madness and Myths

Creative Collaboration

An Introduction to Working with Fathers (with Tony Ivens)

Using the Ugly Duckling to find the Missing Link between Boys and Men

Published by sound of the heart productions and publishers
Copyright 2011
Website: www.soundoftheheart.com

Nick Clements is hereby identified as author of this work in accordance with Section 77 of the Copyright, Designs and Patent Act, 1988. He asserts and gives notice of his moral rights under this Act.

All rights reserved. No part of this book may be reproduced, stored in a retrieval system or transmitted in any form by any means (electronic or mechanical, through reprography, digital transmission, recording or otherwise) without the prior written permission of the publisher.

Photographs and cover design copyright Nick Clements

A catalogue record of this book is available from the British Library Cataloguing in Publication Data

ISBN 978-0-9547302-4-6

Contents

Acknowledgements

Dedicated to the male line which created me. To Richard, my father, blessed be the memory. I am the product of your upbringing, I am indebted to you, I am nothing without you. *I love you, I'm sorry, Please forgive me, Thank you.* I remember the seven generations. To my grandfathers, Harry and Alistaire, and beyond. To my children, Tom and Anna, and all those to come. Thank you Manda for the beautiful children and times we had and continue to have.

I honour those who have helped me with this book, and given inspiration in the creation of it. Rosie and Vanessa, who bravely ploughed through the third version, I am indebted to you. Chris 'Shining Bear' Brosnan, thank you for all the help, support and wisdom. The cover photograph is my dear friend with his newborn son, Fionn. I remember the events and people inspiring this book: the children and staff of Kinderheim Isernhagen in Hannover, Germany to whom I am attached by the umbilical cord of our shared experiences. Sarah and all the other artists from The Pioneers on our journey from 1981 to 2004. Marina, thank you so much for the faith you have in me, for the eldership you recognize within me, which I hide as best I can. Alex, Katja and Rhys at Valley and Vale, thank you for being so kind and for being prepared to support me. Tony, thank you for all the support, for Fatherskills, and the deep discussions we have. To all those men who have supported and encouraged my participation in rituals and ceremonies. To the men who carry the male spirituality bundle, may we all meet, keep in contact, and may we remember who we are – I am inspired by you all. Richard, long may the apples in your orchard bear fruit. Jack, thank you for your fierce ways, for your compassion and for so many lessons. Gabriel, go well in the journey towards the future.

To the Rainbow 2000 tribe, which supports and sustains us all in so many diverse ways. To the memory of Sid Rawles who was inspired and inspiring, with his own unique path to follow. To a great male role model James Carradine who passed away recently, I owe you, you taught me to be myself, to be content with life.

I also remember the friendships enduring through these recent years. Nic and Suzi, thank you. Herewood, may we both continue to enchant the world with our wisdom and stories, you are a gift. Lisa, for your friendship and enquiring ways, thank you. Biddy, thank you for being such a good listener and provider of saunas and food. Maggie, thank you for being so wise and supportive. Nicola, I am still your family – we are connected forever. David, you are a wonderful friend, inspiration and brilliant fisherman – long may we smile at fish together. Malcolm and Clare, thank you for everything that is to come. Vanessa, I love you.

Preface

In 1975 I started working using creativity and imagination, in a children's home in Germany. Since then I haven't stopped. I studied filmmaking and performance, I was a community artist, and I am now a freelance consultant. I am employed all over the world by governments, local authorities, charities, corporations, universities and other institutions. They come with basically the same question: 'These people are ill/unhappy/deprived, can you help them?' I try my best. I use imagination, creativity and play to enable them to gain self-esteem and confidence. I seek to reconnect them to their intuition and inner strength.

Right from the start I tended to work with the boys or men, mainly because I'm a man. To do so is to choose a lonely path – less than three per cent of care or social workers are men. In many situations I have to use my intuition and feel my way forward, as there are no prescribed ways of doing this work. As my understanding and confidence has grown, the complexity and diversity of my work has increased as well. In recent years I have worked with couples, and we explore relationships between men and women. Almost invariably I come across this scenario: the woman asks the man, 'How does that make you feel?' The man replies, 'I don't know.' The reply infuriates the woman, and yet it is a step forward. The man is admitting he doesn't know everything, so there is space for growth. However, enabling the man to recognize his feelings is the next task.

For a long time I have had my head down, doing the work. In the last 10 years this has changed. I am now asked to give talks and show films all over Europe and America. I am a consultant and advisor, not just a worker. This reflects a mood swing in the way we feel about our culture and particularly about men. When I was a young boy, men were the rulers of the world – they made decisions, worked, brought home the money and dabbled in domestic violence and child abuse without any outside interference. Thankfully, things have changed radically. Feminism and our new liberal society have altered men and our ideas of masculinity. The old certainties about masculinity and machismo are no longer so strong. These changes have left a lot of men confused.

As someone who has over 30 years of experience of working with them, I hope I can help. This is a book about men, *for men and women*. It is a map of possibilities. It plots a journey from conception to death. I offer it to you as a gift, a discussion document. It has questions and answers.

Positive Masculinity

To be a man is to perform a balancing act on a wide scale - with the oppressive tyrant at one end and the caring feeling homosexual at the other. My fathers' generation spent most of their time at the tyrant end of the scale. My sons' generation of men will spend much more time at the metro-sexual end. This is a good move, not just for men, but most especially for women and children, in fact, humanity as a whole.

Feminism was a reaction against the tyrant, women wanted to change the balance of power. It has taken a couple of generations for men to react to this change, but they are now slowly coming round to accepting the challenge. Men are in crisis...hurray! For me, this shift can be characterised as a step towards positive masculinity. I am seeking to identify what positive masculinity looks like, and how we can all encourage the next generations to embrace it.

Positive masculinity is a new mindset. It challenges the selfish, materialist model and includes collaboration, mutual aid and support. Positive masculinity is at the forefront of human evolution, and it allies itself with the knowledge that creativity and imagination are the keys to finding the solutions to our present global problems. It links to the concept of us all having a souls' purpose and the importance of spending our lives seeking it, because this brings joy and satisfaction. It also promotes an understanding of the shadow aspects of our culture, and an examination of our past being necessary for change in the future. Positive masculinity allies itself with an increased understanding of our responsibility as individuals and as a species.

Positive masculinity opposes the old tyrant and violent role model, without losing a sense of adventure, challenge, risk and bravery. The new paradigm for men is a diverse, complex and changing form, which encourages them to be both emotionally intelligent and risk-taking. The new man has to experience a wide range of places on the scale of masculinity, and eventually settle at a place which is comfortable for him, but which doesn't impinge on others freedom. This is not a return to any previous state, it is also not a weakening or diminishment of masculinity, it is the development of a new state of mind. It will take time, and such actions will actually strengthen masculinity (and humanity) in the long run.

This book outlines a typical journey from conception to death for a man. It depicts the ages and stages he is likely to undergo, and the rites of passage he may well encounter along the way. I include lessons which link to the rites, and these will engender a specific type of responsible development. In this post-modern culture it is easy to be fearful and cautious about change, but I am seeking to encourage imaginative, risk-taking men who are in touch with their emotions and act out of bravery and responsibility when necessary.

To behave in such ways we will need guidance and assistance, and throughout the book I am keen to support role models, mentors and elders to be present in our male lives. This will ensure some continuity and aspirational development in our young people. We need to encourage our boys to want to become mature men. At present they want to remain forever young. They can see no advantages in growing old. They don't know what ages a man will go through, and how this process can be beneficial. They need to be encouraged to spend time with older men to appreciate how diverse and interesting they can be.

Within the concept of the ages used in this book, we, as a species, are in the later stages of teenagehood. We have spent a lot of time recently asking the question 'why', we are rebelling, kicking and fighting against our parents (the planet).   We now need to step towards responsibility, and realising the consequences of our actions, not blaming others.   As a species we are about to give birth to a new inclusive, compassionate and imaginative mindset.   We all agree the next years will be a rite of passage, and change will affect all of us in a wide range of ways, most of which we won't see coming. In a sense, we now have to step towards the abyss, and have faith that this is the right thing to do.

Let's do it......let's be brave.

I
A Brief History of our Time

I was born in 1956. As a typical product of that age, when I was a young child, I carried brief flickering images in my head about the history of humanity as a whole, and masculinity in particular. I thought these were real, but I was also aware they constituted myths and legends.

Cave men

The cave man, clothed in dark animal skin, hair wild and bearded, large club swung over one shoulder, dragged in his other hand the hair of a reluctant cave woman, who was kicking and screaming as both disappeared into a cave. What would happen in that cave? How those people had relationships, or how they lived, seemed beyond my comprehension. I knew they were wild, uncivilized, without sophistication. They probably ate leaves, raw meat, and had to dodge attacks from dinosaurs. That is how men were in the beginning of 'human time'.

Knights

As time progressed these hairy beasts emerged from their caves, and started to build houses and grow crops. At some point, maybe thousands of years later, men started the concept of 'nobility'. The knight mounted his horse, he rode out into the world, seeking adventures, fighting battles, and vanquishing foes. When he was tired and weary, he turned back to the castle. There his beautiful wife would be tending to the hearth, feeding his young children and anxiously looking out of the castle windows awaiting his return. Once back in the comfort and warmth of his home, the knight laid his weary head on his wife's lap, and she gently stroked his hair and sung him to sleep. He ate, slept, restored himself, and once replete, he rode out on his horse into the wide world. Men did that sort of thing. They went out into the world; women stayed at home.

Conquerors

In the early days of our history, men formed tribes. As we became more sophisticated, we formed villages, towns, societies, and communities. This led us to the concept of 'camaraderie'. King Arthur, Genghis Khan, Attila the Hun, The Greeks, the Romans – all of them believed in camaraderie, and that was how they conquered the world. 'One for all and all for one,' said the four Musketeers. Men went about conquering, the consequence of which was vanquishing, the subjugation of others, which eventually led to our present 'civilization'!

Scientists

After all those battles, wars and fights, men were tired, so they turned their minds to other things. 'Civilization' came about when men began thinking, using logic and science. This started some time before Jesus was born. The Greeks were the fathers of the logical process. Mathematics, which up to this time had been useless, suddenly became important. Things had to be proved, you couldn't believe in something until it had been proven. The only way to prove something was to ask a man in a white coat whether it was true. If he said 'Yes', then it was.

Civilizers

The logical extension of logic... was travel! Men built bigger and better boats, and this allowed us to discover America, Australia and other places in the world where people we didn't know about had been living for thousands of years. This happened about 500 years ago. These indigenous people were supposedly very grateful to us for bringing 'civilization' to them, as they had been practically cave men for many thousands of years. They welcomed us with open arms, and most died of the contagious diseases we brought in that embrace.

Exploiters

Having 'conquered' the planet by war, and then by logic, men set about conquering the planet by farming. We turned the 'wastelands' of America into grain. We ploughed and drove tractors over every part of the planet, bringing strange plants to lands which hadn't had them before, and getting rid of all those untidy and useless forests. Alongside this we replaced those dirty mud huts with nice brick houses.

This progression from cave man to civilized man made sense to me as a child. We were talking about a logical 'ascent of man' – science, technology and capitalism made us more advanced than we were before. As a grown man, I now know most of it was untrue. On occasions it feels more like a descent than an ascent, but these were the ages of man as far as I had been taught. It was a simplistic view of our past propagated in schools and through the media. A more complex and compassionate view of our development is held in the concept of generational intelligence.

2
Generational Intelligence

There have been innumerable generations of man since our inception as a species. Our understanding of what constitutes a generation, and the differences between them, has changed and depends on where we live. In prehistoric times the passing of a generation or culture was a slow process. Dynasties lasted hundreds or thousands of years. In Biblical times the son of the carpenter became the father of a carpenter, and so on for many generations. Nowadays, a radical change in culture and society can occur every 20 or 30 years, and as with everything, we are speeding the process up. The sons of our fathers rarely continue the family tradition; they have separated from their ancestral past, and created something new by the time they reach their early twenties.

This behaviour is fine if each generation learns the lessons of its predecessors. The passing of generational intelligence is the key to cultural progress. The evolution of the human race is dependent on us learning lessons and passing through phases of being. If each generation reinvents the wheel and claims it as new, then progress is slow and we will make the same mistakes over and over again. Sound familiar?

As my father told me, each generation thinks it is the last. We all seek to leave our indelible mark on the world. A generation is defined by its legacy. Almost invariably this only becomes clear as it declines. Its impact on the evolving story of humanity can be identified in a number of ways, namely, by its ideals, behavioural patterns, morals, beliefs, aspirations, the social history of its time and the consequences of its actions. Each generation wants to have been more remarkable than the past, particularly nowadays.

The Beloved

In 2006 I made a film with the semi-nomadic Samburu tribes people of Northern Kenya, who define their culture by the 'Muratare' (circumcision) ritual, which occurs once every twenty years or so. The 106 boys who were circumcised constituted the new generation, and every one of them received the name 'Kishami' (the beloved). The Samburu elders could recite the names of their generations back for hundreds of years.

They recognized that a new generation has little or no influence until the majority of its' number are over 20 years old. At such a stage, its impact on the culture is aspirational, naïve, and often full of principles. When its members are in their thirties to fifties, they create their unique mark and imprint on the culture. This second stage represents the manifestation of their ideals into actions. Then in a sense they become 'kings'; they are in charge. When they reach their sixties and seventies they decline and their influence wanes, but their legacy becomes visible. This third stage can turn one of two ways. A generation which feels it hasn't achieved a great deal can become bitter, and it can stand in the way of progress for the next generation, – actively discouraging change. The lesson is not learnt and not passed on. Or, if its members feel they have achieved something of value, they can now step out the way, and encourage the following generations to continue the work. The lesson is learnt and passed on, and so it goes for many generations. I like the Romany concept of seven generational spirals. It

5

says a new 'first' generation is born at the end of the seventh generation, not an eighth. This allows ties to be broken, behavioural patterns to change and progress to be made; every seven generations we start again.

Like father, like son?

The generation that reached maturation in the 1950s (my father's) was the seventh in a cycle. The first generation of this particular cycle was born at the time of the industrial revolution, and each following generation built on and furthered the industrial revolution. My father's generation was characterized by the security of its beliefs, as are all seventh generations. It was an accumulation of the previous six, a 'solid state' generation. Its' hopes and aspirations were influenced by the Industrial Revolution through to the Second World War and the Cold War. In its time, the man was a powerful beast, and he ruled the roost. The TV series *Mad Men* illustrates the last throws of this generation – smoking, sexual harassment, drinking and domestic violence were acceptable and the norm. Men of this generation typically admired their fathers, and often went into the same industry or work. They represented the continuation of a seven generational ideal that had been passed down to them – materialistic, misogynistic, solid, fixed, aggressive and patriarchal.

Changelings

The next generation of men, the baby boomers, was a 'first' generation. They reached their twenties and thirties in the 1960s and 70s, and here they experienced a great deal more instability than their fathers. This generation is the 'changeling generation'. Typically, the new man didn't like his father. He didn't go into the same work or industry; he created his own. He experienced, supported and participated in the feminist movement of the 1960s, which can be seen as a tipping point for men. Those born to the solid state generation on the whole felt threatened by feminism, and opposed it. Those born to the changeling generation welcomed the change, but didn't have a clue where it would take them.

The first generation always lacks confidence and a map, because it is new, on a new path. The previous changeling generation, at the birth of the industrial revolution, marked the step from a rural and agricultural-based society to a mass-produced, industrial future, and was equally unsure how that would pan out. Huge and immense changes have occurred as a consequence of the choices that generation made, which were unforeseeable at the time.

This present changeling generation have equally significant choices to make, not just about the way in which we all treat the planet, but also about our emotional and spiritual state. We have to introduce true holistic thought and actions. These decisions will be important in the tackling of the present problems, and the future problems for the next six generations; they will be guidelines and signposts. Again, we can not foresee what the consequences our actions will be, but we have to follow our hearts.

3
Help!

The planet is a finite resource.
Humanity is in crisis.
We have multiplied beyond 6 billion, and have conquered the planet.
We are creating stresses and fractures within the fabric of the society we previously felt secure in.
The future is unclear and full of fear.

This can either be a disaster and apocalyptic tragedy, or a wakeup call. For the first time in seven generations or more, human beings are becoming aware of the importance and significance of their thoughts, deeds and actions. The situation has become so dire that even men are in crisis! Men are confused about their identity and how to behave. These insecurities are reflected throughout the generations:
• in the low academic achievement of boys at school, particularly primary schools,
• in the antisocial behaviour and out-of-control attitudes of our teenagers, and the lack of respect they show for society and others,
• in the much higher suicide levels of young men than young women,

- in the numbers of men in demeaning, pointless employment, which creates stress and depression, and leads to petty crime and benefit fraud,
- in the ever-increasing numbers of absent fathers,
- in the continuation of domestic violence and the smacking of children,
- in bitter and resentful old men, not understood or valued, feeling out of place and without purpose.

Crisis inevitably leads to change. Let's not become frozen into inaction by the immensity of the problem; let's change. In this modern age we simplify things. Modern masculinity has been distilled into four ages:

The Kid – the child, the learner, the inexperienced boy who runs around at great speed.

The Lad – the cocky chancer, the leery wide boy, the boozer, influenced by lads' magazines, the petrol head, making money quickly.

The Bloke – the father, the earner, the doer, in employment, in debt, mortgaged, losing his hair.

The Old Git – the miserable man, the complainer, bitter, resentful, out of touch and fearful, doesn't understand and doesn't want to change.

We start out with hopes and aspirations; they are crushed and battered, until we become old and cynical, and then we die. I don't want that to be the template I pass on to the next six generations. I believe men are more complex, and this book is my first step in trying to create a more respectful way of being a man.

Positive and negative

The four ages stated above all move towards negativity rather than positivity. They stress the negative attributes of men and humanity as a whole. Homer Simpson personifies these two aspects. On the negative side, he is an idiot, an inveterate drunk, unable to express his emotions and addicted to fast food and television. Yet, he is also a devoted father, a faithful husband, a provider for his family and a creative inspiration for others. All of us have these two ways of being within us, and at different moments we can be dominated by one or the other. It is not pre-destined, we are not evil by nature, or negative all the time, we have choice. We can choose to step towards the positive rather than the negative.

The history of our recent past is an illustration of the difference between the men who are positively charged, and those who live in negativity. There is a fine heritage of famous men who have lived positive lives, and who surely must be our role models – from Jesus Christ through Mahatma Gandhi and Martin Luther King to Nelson Mandela, men who have questioned the status quo, who have opposed violence, who have promoted love over fear. On the other side, in the extreme, we have individuals who have stepped into leadership through negativity – Alexander the Great, Adolph Hitler, Joseph Stalin and many others. Through repression, they have spread war, violence and created a world full of fear.

Most of us do not reach greatness, or become renowned. Most of us are just foot soldiers in the army of humanity, and on occasions we may be positively charged or negatively inclined, and we believe that doesn't affect the world. It does. All these individuals above are renowned because they had followers; their communality was their ability to inspire and command others. By seeking to live in the positive and to bring about a positive charge in the world we oppose fascism and fundamentalism. By seeking to be positively charged we will create a more holistic, humanistic, compassionate future. There are many men who can be seen as positive male role models or heroes in everyday life. Most of them are unknown and unsung heroes, but just as valid. Some become famous or seek out fame. The media are particularly harsh on heroes – they make them and break them on a regular basis. This means we can often become cynical about role models, and particularly men who are in the public domain. The level of scrutiny they are subjected to makes us aware of how complex they can be. Barak Obama is now a hero for many of us, and the intensity with which he is being observed will be a defining part of his life. I think he has coped extremely well with it. David Beckham has lived with this scrutiny for many years, and has been able to come through many ups and downs. I admire Jeremy Clarkson, not for his views but for his ability to retain his masculinity and to challenge and question the world. They come in all shapes and sizes. I don't have to agree with them, but their flaws make them human and attractive.

Zorba the Buddha

Bhagwan Shree Rajneesh, or Osho, as he was known in his later years came up with the concept of Zorba the Buddha which is a great archetype for masculine development. He starts as Zorba the Greek, from the novel by Nikos Kazantzaki, a larger-than-life character who eats, drinks, womanizes and is very merry. As he grows older, he tires of the superficiality, and realizes something is missing in his life. He is earthly, rooted, like a giant cedar, but he has no wings. He cannot fly into the sky. By questioning his values, he steps towards a different way of being and relating to the world. Zorba the Greek is the foundation of Zorba the Buddha. Buddha arises out of the earth. The comprehension that there is more to life than just the physical creates a yearning for spiritual development. The Buddha uses his earlier life as the foundation for his exploration of the more esoteric nature of the universe. In the next chapters I talk about the eight lessons of men. If we can learn all of these we have a chance of becoming like Zorba the Buddha.

Domestic violence

If there is one product of the old negative ways of being that I am seeking to change, it is prevalence of domestic violence. If the new generation of Zorba the Buddhas can bring about a diminishment of this, then I will be happy. There are no really accurate measures or surveys in terms of domestic violence, as it is still such a closed and difficult subject. In 1995-6 a survey of 16,000 people in America found nearly 25% of women and over 7% of men had been raped and/or physically assaulted by a current or former spouse, cohabiting partner, or dating partner/acquaintance at some point in their lifetime. These are supposedly enlightened and liberated times!

The Duluth Domestic Abuse Intervention Project was created after a violent 'domestic' homicide in Duluth, Minnesota. It focussed on two contrasting wheels of behaviour. The first, the Power and Control Wheel, is based on a negative cycle of control and power that men exert over women. This reflects a great many patterns and learnt behaviours men continue to perpetuate to this day. They are not innate and do not only apply to men. The first wheel can seem difficult to change, but men can do it: If they are assisted and encouraged they will step from the first wheel and enter the second. This is the Equality Wheel, which I believe men can adopt and own, even if they are seemingly caught within the first. If we encourage our boys and men to learn the lessions contained in the ages listed in this book, they will not become trapped in the first wheel, and will live their lives through the second wheel.

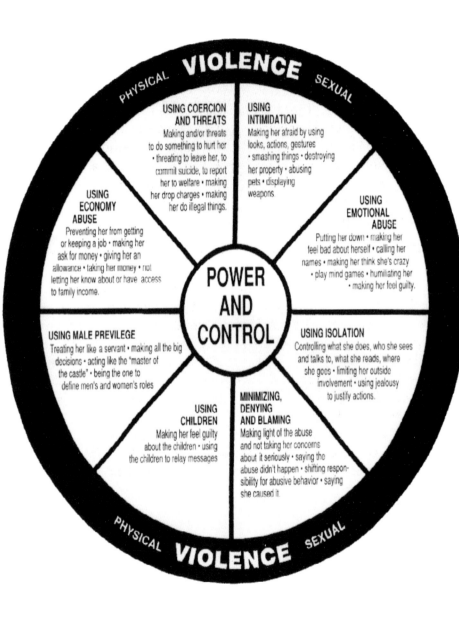

13

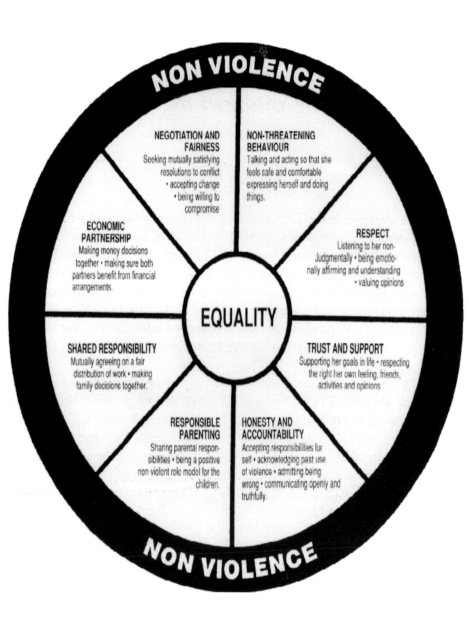

14

4
Creating the new male myth

'For the foreseeable future, men's lives will be caught up in the turbulent confluence of two great mythic systems – one dying, one being born. The old myth perceives reality as constant discord and believes combat, warfare, and economic competition are inevitable; it hopes for clear-cut victories and progress. The new myth perceives life and reality as a unified network of mutually independent entities whose wellbeing is enhanced by cooperation and compassion; it looks forward to a world order not based on warfare, and an economic system that is ecologically viable.' *[1]*

This quote from Sam Keen perfectly sums up the two wheels at the end of the last chapter. The Power and Control Wheel is dying, the Equality Wheel is being born. I take teenagers deep into wilderness. There, they may create sweat lodges, or sit on their own for days. They are encouraged to think and feel deeply, learn about themselves. During these times we are able to form bonds of trust and respect; we talk deeply. The discussions we have always come back to the same point: men don't have to be hard.

Men are hard
Sometime, in our past, we decided men needed to be tough. This is a relatively recent phenomenon, probably only a few tens of thousands of years old. It marked our shift into patriarchy, which is not a fixed state

15

of being. At around the same time, women were given the caring sharer's role. To be honest, not only is this out-dated; it is insulting, and not based on any scientific facts. There needs to be an equality between men and women, and the roles of risk-taker or homemaker are equally important. Men have a slightly higher propensity to take risks, as is shown by the higher car insurance premiums of men. They are physically marginally larger than women. Boys experience a testosterone rush as they grow up; women can give birth and breastfeed. But otherwise, the differences between men and women are very, very small. In these confused times, many people cling to old beliefs for safety and assurance. The old myth of men being strong and women being weak is one of those props. It is no longer needed. Our past does not have to dictate our future. Indeed, our patriarchal past has led us directly to this present crisis-strewn mess. I ask for a little time out, and to start anew; after all, we are a 'first' generation. Maybe we should look a little deeper into our own history to find some help, connect to some of the lessons that were not passed on to us.

Interconnected

The present age of patriarchy is about 20,000 years old. Before that we lived a very different existence, having a reverent and respectful relationship to the planet and nature. Before we started trashing the place, we knew we were related to everything – all the other human beings, all the plants, all our relations. The significance of an individual was not more important than the collective. The destruction of a species was seen as damaging to all species, not just the one. We didn't consider human beings to be better than other species. When we separated ourselves from this web of interconnectedness, we gave ourselves permission to believe we were 'better' than others. We lost our connection to our responsibility to act in accordance with natural laws. Mankind revelled in this new freedom; we went out and either killed it or conquered it, whatever it was – humans, eco-systems, continents, religions, cultures, environments... the planet! Only in recent years have we started to realize the dire consequences, and this has frightened us. Having felt in control and command, we feel suddenly out of control, surrounded by doom and gloom. We have an ecological crisis, an economic crisis, a carbon footprint crisis, a crisis of confidence, a crisis in the high street... you name it, it's in crisis. We are desperately seeking answers, and, for the first time, realizing these may be beyond our comfort zone. The answers may lie away from competition, consumerism, patriarchy. Maybe they include a return to the interconnected collaborator-spirit of our past. Even better to connect the past with the technologies of today. I don't know what the answers are, but I want to make the first steps towards them. We need to find solutions that are truly heroic and radical. This is not the time for caution and trepidation.

Men in crisis

Finally, after thousands of years of ignorant bliss, even masculinity is in crisis. *Hurray!* Men are confused, insecure, bewildered. They no longer know what to do, or how to be men. About time. Many men are still stuck in the negative macho, violent mode, and many do not want to change. Some remain emotionally stunted and unable to express themselves. However, an increasing number of men are prepared for and wanting to change. These rare, precious men need to be encouraged in their positive steps. They have started a change that will radically affect the next generations. They are stepping towards emotional intelligence, non-violence and positive lifestyles. These changes will not affect everyone overnight, but every small victory needs to be celebrated, in order to encourage others.

Remarkably, many women still adhere to the view that a man's place is in charge, and a woman's is in the kitchen. Many other women believe it is not in men's interest to change; they don't believe men want to change. I acknowledge that it is going to be difficult for all of us to bring about positive change. I plead with women as well as men. Let us seek compromises, collaboration and harmony as the templates for the future. I am encouraging a positive view of masculinity, which can replace the old myths. The moment of crisis is the ideal moment to introduce such alternatives.

The ages as set out in this book are a starting point in this change. They are my attempt to take men seriously and not to consider them just as blokes or lads, but as sophisticated and intelligent beings.

Here's hoping!

5
The ages

In 2008 I toured a show about men. I talked about the 7 ages of man because Shakespeare had done something similar. During the course of that tour and in the starting of this book, I have come to the conclusion there are in fact 8 ages. They relate to the eight archetypal experiences during our lives:

- *Conception*
- *Birth*
- *Being able to walk*
- *Leaving home*
- *Having children*
- *Having grandchildren*
- *Being responsible to the wider community*
- *Dying*

These experiences fundamentally influence the development of each one of us – men and women alike. I believe it is useful to use these moments of change as the template on which to construct the new ages. These experiences are archetypes, so you do not need to actually have children in order to learn what it is to be a parent. We all become parents in many different ways. Some of us use the experience of creating a business to simulate parenthood.

19

For each of these experiences there is a name in the development of a man:

- *Foetus*
- *Baby*
- *Child*
- *Teenager*
- *Father*
- *Grandfather*
- *Elder*
- *Death*

Rites of Passage

I will use these names as the titles of each age. There is a natural progression from baby to child, father to grandfather; however, there is also a distinct change at each stage. The baby seeks to walk rather than crawl. When he starts walking he is no longer a baby; he has become a child. This happens each time we move from one age to the next, and I have called these changes 'rites of passage'. Within a rite of a passage there are three stages:

Separation – We become uncomfortable, dissatisfied with our present, and we seek to change ourselves. We separate from the present.

Transition – We learn new skills, ways of being, gain knowledge. We change. We seek a new future.

Incorporation – We recognize that we have changed, we are no longer how we used to be and we act accordingly. We are also recognized as having changed by others.

As we move through the ages we undertake a rite of passage before we can enter the next one. The rite is defined by the lesson we have to learn in order to make progress.

In this book I have used the following lessons for each of the ages:
* *Abundance*
* *Receiving*
* *Exploration*
* *Questioning*
* *Responsibility*
* *Giving away*
* *Forgiveness*
* *Composting*

I have worked with indigenous people all over the world, and with very clever and intelligent people who live in complex, difficult and impoverished circumstances here in Europe. During the course of this work I have been able to ask them about the ages of men, and they have shared their beliefs and thoughts. I have also read many books and texts on the matter, as well as having performed and undertaken many rites and ceremonies myself. My conclusion is that there are archetypal rites through which we have put our men in the past, and that we can learn from them for the future. So I have taken from the past, but also added from the present, with an eye to the future. When I put all this together, it becomes a succession of ages, rites and lessons:

Age	Rite	Lesson
Foetus	Conception	Abundance
Baby	Birth	Receiving
Child	First footing	Exploration
Teenager	Bravery	Questioning
Father	Couvade	Responsibility
Grandfather	Recognition	Giving away
Elder	Supervising	Forgiveness
Death	Recluse	Composting

Ages

The first four ages are focused on learning and growing, the next two are about providing and the last two are just about being. In other words, as children we are focused on the development of self and the creation of our identity, as adults we are more concerned with the care and nurturing of our family (others) and as elders we can be focused on the wider community.

Please remember these are archetypes; don't be put off if you haven't had children, or think it is not necessarily your path to do so. The age of the grandfather is identified by the way in which he acts; he doesn't have to actually be a grandfather. A gay man can easily take on board these ages and rites without having to have children or be in a relationship with a woman, indeed many already do. Life choices do not affect our ability to step through rites and to learn lessons.

Rites and Lessons

I will explain the mechanics of the rite for each age, and how they are a gateway from one way of being to another. They are divided into three stages, based on the definition above: separation, transition and incorporation. The eight lessons relate to the specific needs of the individual at a given time in their development:

The foetus experiences exponential growth and expansion, in size, dimension, understanding, in every way. In a place of 'abundance' the womb, he needs to learn that everything is provided for him.

As a baby the lesson is 'receiving', to enjoy and fully appreciate how to receive from others, as he is very vulnerable.

The lesson from childhood is 'exploration', to be blissfully lost in the wonder of being, exploring the physical universe.

The lesson from teenagers is 'questioning', wanting to learn, to seek more knowledge and wisdom, and stretching the boundaries.

The lesson from fatherhood is 'responsibility', to be responsible for every action taken, every deed, every thought, and being responsible for others.

The lesson from grandfatherhood is 'giving away', to be generous and not to hoard, to understand how to let go of things.

The lesson from the elders is 'forgiveness', not take anything personally, to know life is good.

The lesson from death is 'composting', that everything needs to shrivel and die, everything must come to an end, and by doing so can be transformed into something else.

The next chapters are devoted to the 8 ages. I have broken them into sections.

The rite of passage – through which we have to travel in order to reach the next age.

The lesson – what we need to receive and use in a particular age.

The age – its characteristics, and what we can expect from it.

The age is looked at from a number of perspectives: **past, present** and **future**.

Finally, **suggestions for action are made** – rituals, ceremonies, events and good practice tips.

6

Rite of passage
Conception

The Lesson
Abundance

The Age
Foetus

North East

The colour of **White**
All other colours are held in it

THE FIRST AGE
Foetus

What we call little things are merely the causes of great things; they are the beginning, the embryo, and it is the point of departure which, generally speaking, decides the whole future of an existence. One single black speck may be the beginning of a gangrene, of a storm, of a revolution.
Henri Frederic Amiel

As I said, I toured a show called the 7 Ages of Men, but have since come to the conclusion that there are 8 ages. The age I have added is this one, starting with conception and continuing through the development of the foetus. I have included it because the research I undertook opened my eyes to the amazing journey the foetus takes within the womb.

THE RITE OF PASSAGE
Conception
Separation - *we leave something behind, in this case non-existence*
Transition - *we enter physical reality*
Incorporation - *we start to grow*

Pre-conception
I can't talk about conception without mentioning the importance of pre-conception! The influence of pre-conception on the development of a

human being is immense. Right now we have any number of statistics we can scare ourselves with about the negative consequences of pregnancies. Teenage pregnancies, abortions, absent fathers all are on the increase, and may come about because of trouble in pre-conception.

Teenage Pregnancies

More than 8,000 girls in England and Wales under 16 became pregnant in 2007. Conceptions per 1,000 girls aged 12 to 15 rose from 7.8 in 2006 to 8.1 in 2007. Rates among girls between the ages of 15 and 17 rose as well, from 40.9 per 1,000 in 2006 to 41.9 per 1,000 a year later.

Reasons for abortions

In 2005 there were 820,151 legal abortions in the United States.

25.5% wanted to postpone childbearing

21.3% could not afford a baby

14.1% had a relationship problem or a partner who does not want the pregnancy

12.2% were too young; parent(s) or other(s) object to pregnancy

10.8% believed that having a child would disrupt education or a job

7.9% wanted no (more) children

3.3% were aborted because of risk to foetal health

2.8% because of risk to maternal health

2.1% for other reasons

Absent fathers

According to a US Census Bureau report, over 25 million children live apart from their biological fathers.

Conscious decision-making, information, knowledge and understanding in the pre-conception of a child greatly affect the way in which we then conceive or don't. Fully understanding the consequences of our actions, particularly amongst young fathers, is a priority.

The cauldron

As potential parents, we need to understand we are not the only people participating in the conception. Our families and our families' histories will play their part. Pre-conception is the gathering together of our collective past influences, these will be present at the moment of conception, and exert influence on the future life of the child. These influences may seem abstract, but they can potentially affect the development of the person. They are physical (people, the land, physical circumstances, etc.) and emotional influences (security, fear, love, emotions and feelings).

The period immediately before conception can be a melting pot of love, fear, hatred, lust, pain, drugs, alcohol, ignorance, vanity, war, peace, drought, fecundity and any number and combination of emotions, thoughts and circumstances. Some of those influences we have little or no control over, but others we do. Surely, they need to be founded in love. When I worked in elementary schools in Philadelphia many of the young mothers said they had conceived their child in an attempt to keep their boyfriend interested. They'd hoped the coming of a child would bond them, but often the opposite was true. Conception needs to be motivated by love and a sound understanding of the long-term consequences. It would be ideal if the moment of conception was a perfectly harmonious combination of all the potential influences, and was choreographed by love. The principle of conscious participation by both the mother and father in pre-conception and conception is the ideal. I believe it needs to be discussed openly, and be a part of our frank and honest education for our children in the future. When we discuss conception with young children in schools we mention the biological and physical aspects. This should inevitably lead to a discussion about the mythical, magical and spiritual aspects of the creation of a new life, as well as the societal implications. Within that context we can say pre-conception is a *'Movement of intelligence and life from the infinite,*

eternal, absolute, towards the finite, time, and the relative, for the purpose of manifestation. Life and intelligence come to focalisation. Transformation or descent of life and intelligence so it can express itself as, and through, matter.'
*2

Sounds like a wild adventure, fasten your seat belts!

Sex

I read somewhere that humans are having sex 120 million times a day, *no wonder we're all so tired!* Humans are a quickly proliferating species, and with about 4% of the world's population having sex on any given day, it's no wonder that birth rates continue to increase. Conception doesn't occur every time we have sex, but it is happening on a regular basis all round the world right now. Conception is the start of the journey, which will help us to pursue our soul's purpose, and, hopefully, live the life we were meant to live. In this sense, it is a classic rite of passage – the drawing together of all the influences, their stirring and mixing in the cauldron of the womb, and then the creation, distillation, incarnation of a new individual on a physical journey. The fusion of male and female that occurs in that moment is a wondrous and mystical experience. It is beyond our comprehension. The moment of conception can be felt by the mother and the father – can be appreciated and loved – if we have been conscious in the pre-conceptual stage. The father and the mother bring their contributions, and it is not necessarily the father who brings masculinity and the mother who brings femininity. In the moment of conception everything is possible, and the joining of the two parts creates a new whole.

I have been involved in the conception of two people. I'd love to be able to say that they were conscious decisions, and that I knew what was happening in that moment. My wife, Manda, said she could tell our second child, Anna, was being conceived, and that gives me a lot of hope. My hope is for us to actively seek to encourage conscious conception as an ideal and as a practical experience. I think it would radically affect the levels of participation by fathers in the future lives of their children.

THE LESSON
Abundance
Every person is a God in embryo. Its only desire is to be born.
Deepak Chopra
In the ideal journey into physical existence, once we are conceived, we are perfect. Hopefully, we spend nine months safe in the womb, becoming an individual. The lesson which we need to retain from the process of gestation is that we are conceived into perfection and abundance, our every need and wish is catered for and we grow to a pre-programmed perfection. We are conceived in the fusion of two incomplete parts, so there is magic present. How the joining of the incomplete two creates the perfect one is still a mystery. The process of 'embryogenesis', the making of a whole from the two parts, is not fully understood. Indeed it flies in the face of science – how can two incomplete parts form a whole? Who makes it happen? How do they know what to do? Long may the mystery persist. But it happens – life begins, the human being starts, an individual is created, unique, perfect and full of immense potential.

History lesson
The embryo is taught a history lesson as he grows. This is called 'recapitulation'. As individuals we develop not just in terms of our humanity, but in terms of the evolution of the creatures on the planet. We change from first being a fish, into a bird and finally into a mammal. We experience the evolution of creatures on this planet as we grow,

and we must be learning from this remarkable journey. We have this level of intelligence programmed into us. Our consciousness must absorb these experiences, and who is to know what other messages lie within the experience?

Abundance

Hopefully, in the mother's womb, our every wish and need is catered for. This is not always the case, but it does happen for the majority of us. All the foetus has to do is grow. His mother provides all his food, his nourishment, the disposal of waste, everything, without question, without condition. Unconditional love is the emotion we are conceived into. This experience of individual growth and expansion – the history lessons of recapitulation, the development of consciousness of others and the preparation for life outside water – is a hugely influential experience for all of us. We tend to think of the next stages of the journey from birth to death as the most influential and significant, but they must be all influenced deeply by these first months. In our busy lives, we fuss, we fear, we feel alone. We forget how safe, blessed and loved we were in the womb, and we can continue to be. The experience of the air is no different to the water-borne gestation period, and yet we forget. It would be restorative for all of us if we were to spend time remembering how life was in the womb. We are born into abundance, not lack, and our subsequent abuse of the planet can be traced back to our forgetting of the unconditional nature of gestation. If we can carry the security and knowledge of the experience into our conscious lives, then we would know that we all have enough. Our gestation is in a place of abundance, and the subsequent life is lead on an abundant planet.

THE AGE

Foetus

A baby boy is conceived into an empty and receptive space, and in this damp and dark environment he goes through processes that are so immensely transformative in the creation of his being that they dwarf and make insignificant the changes he undergoes once he is born. This creative process is undertaken in water, secure in his mother's womb. His every need is catered for, he is fed and nurtured, encouraged to grow and stimulated without effort.

Emotional development

To be simplistic, we start out as a backbone. The spine is recognized as the foundation of every one of us, its bones are the first to form and it holds us in place throughout our life's journey. The spine is fixed to the womb and is our contact to the mother. The traumas and events of the gestation period are held in the spine. We take our spines for granted, but when we suffer from minor and major faults, pains, aches and strains throughout our lives, these remind us of the prenatal care we received. If we care for our backs, we are caring for the deep-rooted traumas and fears we experienced in the very early days of our creation as an individual. I know that is a very important message. In many medical and healing practices the concept of the spine relating to the gestation time is well developed and understood. They relate to a journey from the head to the bottom, the neck being the equivalent of the first trimester in the womb, the middle back being the middle period, and the lower back the third trimester.

To further our understanding of this, we need to know what the infant is up to during these times.
*   *The first part of the gestation period, up to 18 to 22 weeks, is spent in the creation of the whole person, which is necessarily an inward process. The foetus is focused on developing himself and his ability to be conscious.*
*   *The period after this, the second trimester, is the change from inward growth to a consciousness about there being others in the world – the 'quickening' which is the opening of awareness to the world. He becomes*

31

aware of his mother as being separate from him, and then the wider influence beyond her.
*   The pre-birth period is the development of the ability to respond to external stimuli. He is getting prepared for action and interaction with the wider world.
A more complete explanation of the trimesters is included at the end of this chapter.

Influences

The relationship between the mother and father has a huge influence on the child – he is more than just a combination of the sperm and egg. The way in which the mother and father relate, communicate and behave influences the development of the foetus, and most especially influences the child once born. For many couples the creation of a baby is the pinnacle of their relationship; it can be the moment that seals and bonds the couple. We need to teach the next generations how to take preconception and conception seriously.

Father

The father's influence is strong during conception. He participates fully in the creation of the new life; he is 50% influential. As the embryo and foetus develops, the influence of the mother increases, but the seed the father has sown is always present. Throughout the rest of this book I will be seeking to encourage fathers to remain as present and as conscious of the significance of their participation as possible. This is not just the responsibility of the father; the mother needs to encourage this, as do we all.

Celestial

The foetus is also influenced by the time of year, that is, by celestial and cosmic changes at the time of conception. We are born into astrological phases, and these influence the lives we lead, despite our scientific distain for such concepts. I spend most of my time giving talks, teaching others, being the focus of attention... oh, that's typical of a Leo, and I was born one.

The era
The developmental stage of humanity, and the world into which we are born, will influence us deeply as well. A child born in 2011 will lead a very different life to a child born in 1911. All of these factors influence us during gestation, not just after birth. The diets of the mothers during the Second World War influenced the growth rates of their children. The baby boom of the 1960s saw a sudden increase in the size and health of the babies, due to the improved diet of the mothers.

THE PAST
Sex and love
The *Karma Sutra,* written between the 1st and 6th centuries, is the first textural exploration of the science of love. Originating in the Tantric school of Hindu philosophy, it attempted to deliver a technical guide to pleasing a sexual partner in a marriage. *The Shuang Mei Ching An Ts'ung Shu* by Yeh Te-Hui, detailing the Taoist concepts of love-making, is probably influenced by them. Both proposed the idea that lovemaking was a natural process, and without pornography, guilt and pathologies, these people were healthy and open in their sexual relationships. The texts came from the educated and rich classes, and reflected their more hedonistic approach to sex and love. By having more free time, the upper classes were able to indulge themselves in such pleasure seeking. The texts noted that the quality of the lovemaking was dependent on the strength of the bond between the couple. The combination of sexuality and sensuality, mental and physical, spiritual and emotional created long-term and abiding relationships. They also advocated lots of practice, which is a good thing! Our own Victorian ancestors were deeply offended by both texts, and really missed the point. Focusing on the pictures rather than the text, they didn't understand that they were

actually very educational and could have helped many couples and individuals at that time.

I have been astonished that men could die martyrs for their religion-
I have shudder'd at it.
I shudder no more.
I could be martyr'd for my religion
Love is my religion
And I could die for that
I could die for you.
John Keats

Keats and his Romantic friends knew how to write about love! At that time, the natural next stage from being in a loving relationship was seen as getting married and the creation of a baby. This was a statement of intent, a confirmation of the love, a blessing on the relationship. Love is a primal instinct, and we all need it. We start out as individuals, but we all seek love, and this comes in the union with another. Love is impossible to define and very personal. The love between two people can assume immense proportions in their lives, can heal, sustain and nurture them and others. The combination of two people in love is a hugely transformative process and can lead people to greatness and peace. It is a powerful tool for change.

Sex can be very different to love. The romantic poem quoted above starkly contrasts with the modern phenomenon of men who are sexual addicts, or who can only undertake one-night stands. These men seek gratification through sex and not through love. They miss out on a lot. A man I worked with led such a life, he actually had notches on his bedpost. One night when both of us were very drunk he tearfully confided in me that he was jealous of my lifestyle. I was together with my wife and we had two small children at the time. He said he'd been rejected by his first girlfriend, and had vowed never to be hurt again. So, he embarked on one-night stands, meeting and leaving women on a regular basis. For the first time, I felt sorry for him, not jealous!

THE PRESENT

Gestation allows the foetus to grow and become conscious of itself and others. The influence of the mother and father is crucial from conception onwards, but the mother does the carrying and nurturing. In this time together the mother can influence the growing foetus:

If she drinks alcohol, uses drugs or eats harmful foods, she is going to affect her child. If she does this on a regular basis the baby may be born into addiction or with health difficulties.

If she is exposed to danger, is fearful or anxious or is violated or beaten, these terrible experiences will be felt and comprehended by her baby.

If she suffers mental torment, is oppressed or feels neglected, sad or depressed, the baby will experience it too.

If she lives in a world of war, violence, want and need, lacks water and sanitation or doesn't eat enough, the baby will suffer with her.

Too many women live in these kinds of places, experience these kinds of treatment, know the truth of this situation, right now on this planet. It is our duty to change such circumstances, such situations. We all have a responsibility to ensure that women can carry the next generations in peace, harmony and love. We need to ensure that the future generations are carried in love and positive support. Even given these circumstances we are still bringing some very remarkable and wonderful people into the world, and they will be working towards the positive future.

THE FUTURE

Everything you need you already have. You are complete right now, you are a whole, total person, not an apprentice person on the way to some place else.
Wayne Dyer

We are perfect when we are conceived, we have everything we need right from the start. As we go on our journey we are, at any given moment in time, perfect; we can't be anything but. We live in an abundant world, surrounded by love; we always have and we always will. In this sense, we do not develop, we can't; we already are complete. To understand this, is to live to your full potential. In the moment of conception we ask the question 'Who am I?' We spend the next years searching for the answer. We spend a lot of time seeking completion, trying to find who we are, and what we came here to do. The paradox is that the answer resides within us, and always has. We come into the world complete. But, the journey, the life that we seek to live, is there to be enjoyed and lived to the full.

SUGGESTIONS FOR ACTION
Conception
A baby is for life, not just for Christmas. Please consider this. Some couples have problems conceiving, others find it not difficult at all. Conception should be a beautiful act. It should also be fun and enjoyable. A woman is more likely to conceive if she has an orgasm during sex, so men need to be good and attentive. Practice what the *Karma Sutra* preaches – do it lots of times. Most of all relax and be grateful. The creation of a new life is a precious gift.   If the father can be conscious of the moment of conception, then I think this will influence his future behaviour, and encourage him to be positive and participate more fully.

Growth charts
Once the baby has been conceived and is starting to grow, it is difficult to picture what he is like or how he is developing, especially for the father. He is just confronted by a bump on his partner. Whilst working with young fathers, I created a 'growth chart' for the baby. This was a

simple version of the changes in the development of the baby within the mother's womb. Similar to a measuring chart for children, it can be ticked and read by the parents. The fathers and mothers, found it very useful, and it made them appreciate the development of their baby. Another benefit arose within families with existing children. The children found it fascinating to know when their future brother or sister was growing fingernails, or able to smell, etc. They also became much more respectful of the mother, and paid a lot more attention to the new bump. Research shows that the bump can recognize different voices, so it is very important that the father and older siblings talk to it, and familiarize themselves with the bump before the baby arrives. The growth charts were based on the developmental stages as outlined below in the trimesters.

The Trimesters

There are three trimesters or stages of pregnancy. Each trimester is 12 to 13 weeks long. Each marks a different phase of development for the baby and different types of challenges for the expectant mother.

Trimester I
From week one to week thirteen

The heart begins to beat with the embryo's own blood, often a different type to the mothers'. By the end of third week the spinal column and nervous system are forming. The liver, kidneys and intestines begin to take shape. By the end of week four the embryo is ten thousand times larger than the fertilized egg. Eyes, legs and hands begin to develop. Brain waves are detectable; mouth and lips are present; fingernails are forming. Every organ is in place, bones begin to replace cartilage and fingerprints start to form. By the 8th week the baby can begin to hear; he also becomes sensitive to touch. Teeth begin to form, fingernails develop. The embryo can turn his head. The embryo becomes a foetus. He can 'breathe' amniotic fluid and urinate. By Week 11 he can grasp objects placed in his hand; all organ systems are functioning. He has a skeletal structure, nerves and circulation. The foetus has all of the parts necessary to experience pain, including nerves, spinal cord and thalamus. Vocal cords are complete.

Trimester 2
From week fourteen to twenty seven
The foetus has an adult's taste buds. Bone marrow is now beginning to form. The heart is pumping 25 quarts of blood a day. By the end of month 4 he will be 8–10 inches in length and will weigh up to half a pound. He can have dream (REM) sleep. He recognizes his mother's voice. The foetus practices breathing by inhaling amniotic fluid into his developing lungs. He will grasp at the umbilical cord when he feels it. Most mothers feel an increase in movement, kicking and hiccups from the foetus. According to the Endowment for Human Development, studies suggest a baby can detect odour at 26 weeks after fertilization. Eyes begin opening around the 26th week and pupils can detect light and dilate by the 33rd week.

Trimester 3
From week twenty seven onwards
His entire body can feel heat, cold, pressure and pain. Eyeteeth are present. The foetus opens and closes his eyes. He is using four of the five senses (vision, hearing, taste and touch.) He knows the difference between waking and sleeping, and can relate to the moods of the mother. The baby's skin begins to thicken, and a layer of fat is produced and stored beneath the skin. The transition from bump to baby is the next change in the development of the man, and in order to do this, we need to be birthed from the world of water into the world of air.

Breathe deeply my little brave one.

7

Rite of passage
Birth

The Lesson
Receiving

The Age
Baby

*The colour of **yellow***
Dawn of a new day

East

THE SECOND AGE
Baby

If one feels the need of something grand, something infinite, something that makes one feel aware of God, one need not go far to find it. I think that I see something deeper, more infinite, more eternal than the ocean in the expression of the eyes of a little baby when it wakes in the morning and coos or laughs because it sees the sun shining on its cradle.
Vincent Van Gogh

When my two children were born I was amazed at how worldly-wise the little fellows already were. Until the birth of my son I'd not really come into contact with babies, and I presumed they would be delicate, squealing, red-faced fragile little beings. They were indeed tiny and reliant, but they were also incredibly durable and resilient. Spending time with both of them made me realize just how wise babies are, how we need to respect them for their innate wisdom and listen to them carefully. They come into the world as teachers as well as pupils.

THE RITE OF PASSAGE
Birth
Separation – *The baby separates from the womb, water and oneness*
Transition – *He literally moves from confinement to vastness*
Incorporation – *He experiences the world beyond the womb, he becomes aware of others*

At the moment of birth, he is assisted out of water and into air, a very different environment, which can feel very intimidating. The close proximity of the womb is replaced by the vastness of the universe. This comes as a shock. Suddenly, he has to inhale air, to make his own way in the world. All of us go through this rite of passage, and it remains probably the most dangerous of all rites we undertake. Those babies who've been part of a peaceful, calm birth process, where the mother has remained relaxed and was well-supported, will recover quickly from the shock of entering a new world. Those babies who've experienced trauma, pain for the mother, stress and worry, will take longer to recover. The innate resilience of the baby means they will recover and continue with life; however, the trauma or beauty of the experience will remain with them throughout their lives. Along with the experience in the womb, birth and the next part of his journey are the keys to the development of a healthy adult.

Babies are incredibly complex and delicate beings, but their needs are very simple. They need to be fed, cleaned and held, but even more importantly they need to be loved. Attachment happens at this early stage; his connection to his mother and father affects the development of his brain. Boy babies need as many cuddles and as much love, affection and care as girls. By receiving this they feel at ease and will grow healthy and happily; the latest toys and outfits mean nothing.

THE LESSON
Receiving
The newborn baby is defenceless and totally reliant on others. He intuitively makes it worth other people's while to give to him. He is so good at receiving – it is, after all, his only skill – that he actually gives to others whilst receiving. This is an important lesson for all of us. I train primary school teachers, the great majority of whom are women. (I encourage their use of creativity and increase their self-esteem.) They are on the whole well practiced in the art of giving – they serve their children, their families and their communities, but they often receive little or no praise, and do not accept it well. They are very embarrassed and almost resentful when receiving. They seem flustered and don't know how to receive well, that is, graciously and with enthusiasm. They need to remember how to receive as well as to give. All too often they believe it is selfish and self-centred to receive; this is incorrect.

Breastfeeding
Babies teach us how to receive gracefully and with gusto. When we do this, we overcome all resentment in the giver. The baby can do nothing other than receive and in so doing he can actually assist the giver. This is illustrated in the cycle of baby and mother. The breast which is offered, the milk which is drunk, the baby who finds satisfaction in the feeding, the mother who feels proud of her son – these are mutually supporting spirals. The baby can be fed by a bottle, but the baby is not feeding the bottle in return. The true nature of a baby learning how to receive is in his comprehension of the push me–pull you of the experience, the reciprocity. A mother who feeds her baby with a bottle receives a great deal less from this lesson.

The baby needs the assistance of parents, his family and the wider community in order to make it from being a baby into being a child. He gives his own unique gifts to each of them by just being a baby. He gives us all a huge lesson in unconditional love and positive regard, the essential prerequisites for a well-adjusted life. The baby is perfect as an example of self-awareness.

THE AGE
Baby
Welcome to the world, little wise one. What a baby does by being born is he challenges and dramatically alters the lives of those around him. He mixes us up. He unconsciously asks some very severe questions of us. When I work with young fathers I often say that my son being born was the equivalent of suddenly waking up and finding myself naked on the central reservation of a very busy motorway. The gift of his birth, and subsequently that of my daughter, left me feeling completely helpless, exposed and vulnerable. All my previous experiences and knowledge was valueless. My children taught me to grow up, to become responsible, but also to own my fallibilities.

Relationship
By its very nature the gestation of the baby in the mother's womb leaves the father relatively unaffected. Nowadays the inclusion and active participation of the father in the birth and beyond, his active encouragement and support for his partner, will all mean he becomes involved and aware of the progress being made. I think his presence at the birth is essential, not only for the mother and the child, but also, most especially, for him. He needs to be aware of what is happening, and to feel responsible for the changes occurring in his life. The old fashioned way – the father presented with a wrapped and swaddled baby onto which he can smile, is not enough. We need the father to bond with his child by being involved and feeling welcome. Typically, the relationship between the mother and the baby, especially in the first

months, can be intense. This can be a challenge to the mother/father relationship, although this is not always the case. The mother is, hopefully, thrown into a deeply mutual loving relationship with the baby. She breastfeeds and caters for all his needs, and there is little or no time for the father. This can cause insecurity and resentment in the father. The mother and the baby become the focus of attention for the family and wider community. They are showered with gifts, given attention, love and affection. Often the father can be sidelined and feel excluded.

Hard work

Any cracks or flaws in the mother/father relationship can be stretched and accentuated in these early months of the baby's life. These are stormy times. The first-time parents of a baby are almost inevitably confronted with sleep deprivation, and they really understand what it is like to have someone completely dependent on them. Tiredness leads to anger and arguments, and the modern family, seeking to return to normal (work) as soon as possible, can be a fraught arena. The taking of maternity and paternity leave is essential at this time. This needs to be spent together as a family as much as possible. Many parents talk about the creation of a 'nest', a safe space into which the mother, father and baby can retreat. This space is theirs, and theirs alone, created with love and developed to nurture and enhance love.

Communication before, during and after

Obviously, discussion and communication needs to be present during these times. The new demands should have been discussed before the birth, so both partners are aware and ready (as best they can be) once the birth occurs. Such stresses can be lessened if the father has been more active during the gestation time as well. The chapter on fatherhood will discuss the use of 'couvade' as a rite of passage for the father, which addresses the need for him to bond to the child. If bonding is difficult or not happening, then we need to take action, some of which could be:

- *The mother can leave him in charge of the baby on a regular basis*
- *He needs to receive congratulation and praise*
- *He can change nappies right from the start*
- *He should hold and cuddle the baby as often as possible*
- *His opinion should be sought and valued*

We can't force the father to bond with the baby, but we can give him as many opportunities to participate as possible.

Many of the young fathers I work with are in a state of shock immediately after birth. Typically, they haven't changed their lifestyle during gestation; they still go out on a regular basis. They don't like the change in the shape of their partner and the subsequent changes in her attitude towards sex (not wanting so much), going out (not so interested), and lifestyle (not working). Some are reluctant to participate in the birth, which can be a traumatic experience, filled with blood and screams. Suddenly, they're at home with a partner they don't recognize and a tiny baby who screams all the time. They are confused, angry and tired, and can feel very resentful towards the baby. Enabling the healing and bonding of their relationship to their partner and baby can take some time. I know this experience is now no longer typical for all of us, but it is still happening and we need to seek to change this for the benefit of future generations.

Physical development

Babies are, pound for pound, stronger than an ox. Although now growing more slowly compared to when he was a foetus, the baby still develops faster at this stage than at any other in his life to come, changes and physical development can almost happen overnight. The average child develops a control of his limbs by 4 months, is able to sit by 7 months and by 9 months is crawling and exploring.

Social development

During the first two months of the baby's life, most of his attention will be focused on his prime carer(s). Around 3 months, the 'social smile' will appear. It's not until after 6 months that the baby will be able to distinguish his prime carers' faces in any given circumstances. By 7 months he'll be smiling at everybody he recognizes.

Cognitive development

The two most important achievements in cognitive development will be the discovery of 'self' and the realisation that objects have permanence – they still exist even when he can't see them. Both these discoveries will happen around 6-8 months. It's that look of amazement on a baby's face when he pulls his own toe, and realizes there is a connection – the hand, the toe, himself, they're all one.

Emotional development

In his first two months, he will mostly react positively when comforted and very negatively when in pain; don't we all! Often, babies will start crying more after 6 weeks and around 3 months go through a tough period. At 4-6 months the boy will begin to regulate his emotions better and may seem like a different baby. He will always enjoy being cuddled. He will be possessive towards his prime carers until about 9-10 months. During this phase, he will usually become distressed when separated from them. This 'separation anxiety' is normal and sign of a healthy attachment.

THE PAST

Before the invention of prams and wheelchairs, babies were carried at all times, strapped, not necessarily to their mothers, and carried around. There was no alternative. They watched the world from the safety of a held place. Whilst being held, he was taken to work, he saw the everyday interactions of people and he was introduced slowly and respectfully into the wider community. By being held and being shown the world he was slowly weaned from dependency and allowed to interact more fully with the wider world. He then reached a time in his life when he was ready to be put down, to take his first steps in the world and to interact in a new way that was unrestricted and not held. He stepped from being a baby to a child, but before he did that he needed a name.

Naming

The most important ritual for a baby is his naming. The giving of a name to a baby represents a long-term commitment to parenting, and should be done with respect and ceremony. In Judaism, the naming of the child is of great significance, and special naming ceremonies, or 'Simchat Bat' are held for the girls. For the girl, this is the father making a blessing on the Torah for the health and wellbeing of his daughter and wife. The boys are not so fortunate! On the eighth day the son is subjected to 'Brit', the ritual circumcision by a Mohel who normally does the work early in the morning. The traditional understanding of the circumcision is that it represents his naming; the name is literally cut into his flesh, and he then has a sign of the covenant in him. The circumcision is also a very potent symbol of the ancestral past, connecting the baby, through his penis, to the future generations to come.

In Indonesia and Malaysia babies were traditionally treated differently. When the baby was born they recognized he had connections to his placenta, which had accompanied him in the womb. The placenta was called the 'Anggi' – the little brother/sister. After wrapping the placenta in a bag of leaves, the husband was instructed to bury the bundle in a deep hole, so no animals could dig it up. (If they did, the baby would constantly cry because of the pain from his Anggi.) The midwife protected the spiritual growth of the baby by rubbing chewed betel nut onto his fontanelle. The mother was confined with the baby, and visited by her family and community at all times of the day and night for the next seven days. This enabled her to bond correctly with the baby, and by doing so encourage the baby's soul, or life force, to connect to his physical body. They believed in these first days that the baby remained close to death, as the life force was not strongly connected. The husband was confined to the house as well. His job during this time was to keep the fire going; the friends and family provided all the food and drink. If the child survived the 7-day confinement then he was named on the next day. As part of the ritual feast and ceremony the naming ceremony was not only for the baby; the parents received their first baby's name as well.

THE PRESENT

Caesareans

To give birth is one of the wonders of the world. It is an extremely dangerous and beautiful thing. There is a conundrum within our society when it comes to giving birth and it relates to the risks involved. We live in a litigious society, as a consequence of this caesarean births have been on the increase in the last few years. The increase seems to have been driven by concerns about liability rather than the health and wellbeing of the mother and child. Recently, it came to light that an obstetrician who practiced in a hospital in the south of the USA had maintained a caesarean rate below 10% for more than a decade, yet instead of receiving accolades for this, she faced difficult demands from the hospital's staff and administration. She not only maintained caesarean birth rates lower than the rates suggested by state and national recommendations, but also attained a high percentage of mothers with gestational ages of 39 weeks. Under her care, infants had higher birth weights than infants from other obstetrical practices in the same community. Additionally, her practice exhibited no indication of higher mortality or morbidity rates among her patients when compared with other local practices. With improvement of the preterm birth rate and low birth weight being a national priority, this obstetrician should have been honoured. Instead, her obstetrical colleagues and the administration of the hospital told her that, in a 6-month period, she must raise her caesarean rate to a level within two standard deviations of the mean for that hospital – a mean that is higher than both the national rate and the rate for the state in which the hospital is located. For this physician, the increase would have resulted in a caesarean rate of at least 20%. We have started to lose contact with the innate beauty and wonder of birth. If the mother is happy, content, at ease and, relaxed, then the likelihood of there being problems at birth is greatly reduced. If she is in a hospital, an environment she doesn't know, if she is tense, stressed and anxious, there are more likely to be complications.

Being held

Babies need constant and undivided attention, especially in the first weeks. He will miss the warmth and comfort of the womb in which he was resident for 9 months. It is very unlikely that he will adjust and cope with such dramatic changes in less than 4 to 6 months. This is not a great deal of time in the overall scheme of things, but all too often our babies do not receive sufficient love and attention at this time. They are left for long periods on their own, without human contact, which can be extremely damaging psychologically. They are ignored and can be shouted at, or experience anger. For any baby this is wholly unexpected, and wholly unacceptable – no baby can ever comprehend anger.

Consequences of not enough baby time

The great majority of us didn't receive sufficient 'baby time' before we were asked to move onto the next age. Almost all the people of the western world were asked to be children before they had experienced enough of being a baby. They weren't held all the time; many were not breast-fed; they were abandoned and left on their own; they were chastised irrationally. These things can cause untold and deep-rooted damage. We all carry the psychological scars, and they add to the potential damage that occurred in the prenatal experience. This means, given the opportunity, the great majority of us want to revert back to being babies. This manifests itself in a variety of ways, most of which are corruptions of that original concept of receiving.

*   *Our selfishness, the focus on our needs above those of others. Because we weren't babies for long enough we are still seeking selfishly, not from a place where giving is equal to receiving.*

*   *Our desperate need to be secure, insulated, centrally heated – a distant echo of the baby seeking warmth and comfort. We overheat our homes, we build ridiculously complex houses and we insulate our lives in many ways.*

*   *Our belief that we are better and more 'grown up' when we stand alone. Self-made men are hard, lonely and bitter. They need to realize that reliance on others is actually a good thing.*

*   *Our fixation on breasts, and their customization which comes with plastic surgery. Some of our men are still looking to receive the breast, a confusion between sexuality and mothering.*

THE FUTURE

We need to remember quite how important the first few months are in determining the eventual adult. The breastfeeding of babies needs to come back into fashion. Men must share the task of holding and being with the baby. It is essential to the baby's and his own well-being. Over a thousand years ago, Larus the bard told the story of Aitor, the founder of the Basque people. He described a practice in Spain that continued through to the 1860s: *"And thus, when a young mother leaves her bed of confinement, her husband at once takes her place with the newly-born child, so that, by its inhaling the manly and paternal breath, the strength of the small and puny being is endowed with sympathetic influence."*[*3] Along with the Basque people, Central Europeans, Americans, Africans and Indians all recognized and recorded how important it is for the baby to smell and taste his father in those early days. This is not just about the baby; it is also about the father. It is an evolutionary imperative that he bonds with the baby, and what better way to encourage it than by giving him the baby and letting him stay with it.

Paternity leave

We need to ensure that paternity and maternity leave is focused entirely on the needs of the baby. The amount of time we allow the father to share with the newborn child is often an indicator of how important we feel the father's role is within parenting. Paid paternity leave in Britain is for two weeks, in Sweden it is 16 months – need I say more? We must encourage the parents to take this leave seriously, and to confine themselves as part of this process. They do not have to care for the baby alone; indeed, a great many of our present problems stem from a belief that parents should do this work alone. They need support. They need grandparents, midwives, fellow parents and their other children to share and give to the baby. Many of the young families I work with in the South Wales valleys have extended families living nearby. Often the parents will say the grandparents have been their saviours in terms of looking after the baby and taking over. Many say the extended family saved their marriages and relationships by enabling them to take time and space together.

Some of the minimum requirements for a baby are:
* *To be in contact with a human being as often as possible*
* *To be fed as and when he needs*
* *To be breastfed if possible (breast milk can immunize him against diseases)*
* *To be cherished and loved*
* *To be praised and welcomed into the world*
* *To be named*
Some of us have lost contact with these minimum standards, and by doing so we have begun to fail our babies. It is time to allow our babies

the fullness and complete experience that ensures they are ready and willing to move onto the next age, being a child.

SUGGESTIONS FOR ACTION
Fathers talking to each other

It is encouraging that so many fathers are now present at the birth of their child: 98% of fathers attend the birth, 48% attend antenatal/parenting classes, 85% attend at least one prenatal appointment with a midwife, and 86% at least one ultrasound scan (National Health Service, 2005). This level of participation should be maintained. However, in my experience many of these fathers are left traumatized by the experience. I am now running workshops with midwives for both partners before birth. At these events I work with the fathers to discuss on a very deep and personal level their fears and worries, their prejudices and their concerns for the future. These frank and often angry sessions enable the prospective fathers to really understand what they are preparing for. They are not tokenistic or impersonal. They are attended by a mix of prospective first-time fathers and experienced fathers. Almost invariably, the first-timers are very grateful and appreciative of the frankness and openness of the other fathers. This may seem like shock tactics, but it is one way of preparing them, and we do focus a lot on the positive as well as negative aspects. During the weekends we separate the men from the women. Safe within these all-male environments we discuss very personal subjects. We have touched on the common misconception that having penetrative sex will somehow damage the baby, easily dismissed as bragging about the size of the penis. We talk about the ways in which the changes in the partner can affect the man, sometimes making her attractive, sometimes less attractive. We discussed the urge to taste the partner's milk, and how one father became so obsessed by it that he would refuse the children access to his partner's breasts. Some of the other things we have discussed I won't put to print!

Honouring the placenta

The placenta is the foetus's lifeline. It supplies nourishment and oxygen from the mother to the foetus. It draws and disposes of the foetal waste, and delivers it to the mother. It produces oestrogen, progesterone and gonadotrophin for the foetus. Basically, without the placenta, the foetus would not survive. Even the delivered placenta is a diagnostic indicator for illness and disease in the newborn child, and can provide crucial information. As discussed earlier, many cultures honour the placenta. The Nepalese think of the placenta as a friend of the baby's and encourage dialogue between the two. Similarly the Malaysian Orang Asli think of it as the baby's older sibling. The Maori of New Zealand give the placenta a burial in honour of its work. The Kwakiutl of British Columbia bury the girls' placentas to give her clam-digging skills, and leave the boys' placentas on the bare rocks to be eaten by ravens and enable the boy to receive future prophetic visions. The Ibo of Nigeria consider the placenta to be the deceased twin of the baby, and conduct full funeral rites for it. Native Hawaiians believe that the placenta is a part of the baby, and traditionally plant it under a tree, which then grows with the child. Increasingly, there is an awareness of the significance of the placenta, and this is being acknowledged here in the West as well. I think we should look at these examples and adapt them.

Naming ceremony

I gave the example of the Judaic Brit ceremony earlier. This comes from a particular tradition, and has been carried through to the circumcision rites for teenagers, which I will describe later. Naming my children was enough for me! The Christening ceremony is a confirmation of the coming of a baby, and welcomes him into the wider community. Quite often, the first days of a baby's life are spent within the close-knit family, so the naming ceremony is a chance for the baby to be acknowledged by the wider community. I think that is a very beautiful and splendid way of allowing the baby to spread his influence. I have been part of many naming ceremonies – some deep in the woods, with the baby being introduced to the fairies and spirits as well as the humans; some simple blessings with water and the bringing of personal gifts; some with commitments from Godparents to the baby for the future. The most moving by far was for a baby who died within the first weeks of life. The depth of emotional expression, the quality of the singing and laments, the decoration of the tiny coffin – all will remain with me for as long as I live.

8

Rite of passage
First footing

The Lesson
Exploration

The Age
Child

The colour of **Orange**
The rising sun

South East

THE THIRD AGE
Child

If I had influence with the good fairy who is supposed to preside over the christening of all children, I should ask that her gift to each child in the world be a sense of wonder so indestructible that it would last throughout life.
Rachel Carson

In 1998 we made a huge mosaic mural with over 150 local children in Jaipur, India. They ranged from 4 to 18 years old, from uniformed private schoolchildren to raggedly-clothed kids who had lost limbs. We worked for 5 weeks to design, make and mount the mural onto an exterior wall of a hospital. Having been used to the indifference of children from Europe, I was amazed by these children. How enthusiastic they were. How we could laugh and share stories without knowing each other's language. How patient and calm they remained. How joyful and full of fun they all were. One boy, about 10 years old, who had no arms, came and watched me whilst I cut the ceramic tiles with very strong metal clippers. I'd instantly made a judgment about whether he could participate fully in the process. I'd decided he'd only be able to watch and encourage the others. After cutting a tile, I lay the cutters down on the floor. He instantly reached over with his foot and picked the cutters up in his toes. He pushed his other foot down onto a tile, manipulated the cutters so he could grip it, and then cut it with no problem at all. What do I know about children!

THE RITE OF PASSAGE

First footing

Separation – *The baby separates from being held, being carried, being dependent*

Transition – *He contacts the earth, is able to move freely on his own*

Incorporation – *He connects to the wider community beyond his own family*

If we have paid attention to him, our baby is now desperate to go out into the world, to be interactive, not passive. He has had his fill of being fed and held, and he is ready and willing to take his first steps on his own. We need to acknowledge he is no longer a baby; he has become a child. The best way of doing this is to create a rite of passage for him. I found many celebrations in the Far East linked to this age. I call these 'first footing' celebrations. They involve literally putting him on the ground for the first time. This is a huge change, not only for the child, but also for the parents. Up till this point the baby is dependent on others to carry him from place to place; now he is being encouraged to make his own way.

First steps

The child taking his first step is always a milestone event, recorded in the minds and memory, and most especially the cameras, of all parents. The day the child walks, the Malays carry out the 'Turun Tanah' or 'coming down to earth' ceremony. The child will step down a sugar cane ladder. This symbolizes him coming down the steps or ladder from the kampong house to the ground. The kampongs are built on stilts, and can only ever be entered through the ladder. With our increasing influence, most Malays no longer live in kampongs. Instead of coming down the steps and landing on 'earth', the boy now lands on a plate of *Bubor Merah Bubor Puteh*, a sweet rice pudding, symbolising a sweet and happy journey in life for the child. In Indonesia, they perform a similar ceremony called the 'Tedak Siti', or 'first step' ritual. Again, the boy is ritually helped down a ladder, but this time into a bath. The ceremony is believed to connect him to the legendary birth of Siddhartha (the Buddha), at which nine dragons washed the baby with perfumed water provided by the gods. On the date of the Buddha's birthday this event is celebrated with the ritual bathing of a statue of the baby Buddha. He is surrounded by flowers, to symbolize Lumbini Park, where he was born. The baby is bathed in five coloured and fragranced waters: blue symbolizing refuge; yellow for wisdom; red for compassion; white for purity; and black for aspiration. Each participant pours water over the head of the baby, and makes vows. Some bring this water back home with them and they let every member of the family drink from it, because the water has attained 'virtue' through the ceremony. What a beautiful and meaningful way of commemorating our child's first steps in the world. Unlike the previous rite, birth, the risk around this second rite is minimal, but that shouldn't deter us from making a fuss, and commemorating such an important change, not only in his life, but the lives of all those around him.

THE LESSON
Exploration

The child who has been through his first footing is able to walk, run and jump. Children explore the world, and one of the most delightful aspects of this is the way in which they see ordinary and extraordinary events and objects for the first time. When they see a butterfly it can transfix them, and they frequently express wonder and awe at this and other such moments. To be around a child who expresses wonder is to be given a huge amount of joy. Exploration is the essence of childhood, and the child must be encouraged to express and share his wonder. The parents may guide and supervise the child in his exploration, but they need to do this in a way that stimulates and encourages wonder. The parent who suppresses wonder and exploration – 'Don't touch that, it's dirty', 'Oh, that's just a bug', 'Yes, we all know it's a car.' – is letting their children down. Their negativity is promoting cynicism, fear, pessimism and oppression, and they are forcing their children to grow up in a fearful way. We must allow our children to explore and be in wonder for a long time, and not encourage them to be grown up too soon. Part of that growing up has to be spent experimenting, and as a consequence of this, children get things wrong, they make mistakes. If, as adults and parents, we either don't allow our children to make mistakes, or we punish them, we are failing them. Children need to make mistakes in order to learn, none of us get it all right.

Living in the now

My own memories of childhood include moments of lucidity around being in nature, observing caterpillars, touching beetles, feeling the earth, being in awe of a mole, appreciating the sun. Unlike other memories – school, work, special events - they don't have a time frame, a date or a reason attached. They are just sensations, images, feelings, emotions. These are the blissful moments we need to engender in our children, and to allow them to experience without interference, fear or judgment. The memories take me back to a phase in my life when I had no concept of time. Allied to the sensations and remembered images, there is a sense of timelessness; not of time standing still as such, but just being unimportant, irrelevant and not present. In those moments we are truly present, we are truly in the 'now'.

The age of childhood teaches adults important lessons. We live stressful and busy lives, and by doing so we exhaust our minds and bodies. We also try to extract meaning and significance from everything we do. Many people I work with can't see the importance of spending time 'doing nothing'. If they are not making money, looking after the family,

59

being responsible, taking care, then they can't see the point of it. This is a sad state of affairs for a human being. If you can't see why we should all spend some time, preferably every day, doing some creative, playful, awe-inspiring activities, then the society you live in is corrupt. The recuperative values of creativity and play are well documented in scientific treaties from around the world. Remembering that we need to restore our play/work/life balance will enable us all to live longer, be happier, generate more wealth, live fulfilled lives, make friends, maintain relationships and so many other things. Trying to return to play and wonder as frequently as possible will nurture and enhance our lives.

Managing play and creativity

I am employed by companies and corporations to enable their CEOs and managers to play. My workshops challenge these clients to draw, write poetry, play with bricks, design beautiful mosaics, sing together. The resistance to these activities can be very strong and many people find these simple workshops challenging in the extreme. They feel embarrassed and think the activities are 'childish', and those resisting the most inevitably ask 'Why am I doing this?'   They're doing it for a multiplicity of reasons, some of which are as follows:

* Often they will be asking their staff to undertake simple and straightforward tasks. Their staff may well resist and be unable to perform them. I am enabling them to remember what that resistance feels like. For me, the activities I'm asking them to perform are simple, very basic, and yet they find them difficult.

* By resisting and feeling foolish, they are able to break through their own barriers and resistances to creativity and play. Once through, they really participate and enjoy themselves.

* Creative and playful activities will stimulate our imaginations and enable us to use the right side of our brains more easily.

* Play and creativity are always about problem solving. The pile of jumbled bricks becomes a house by arranging them. This is a very useful transferable skill for managers, all of us indeed.

The parents of a child need to provide a consistent and balanced home environment in which he can develop his social skills. In order for him to do this he needs to be encouraged, praised, challenged and respected. We must understand that the child should be seen *and heard*. The child must be able to express himself in his own unique and imaginative way, and we need to listen to and encourage him in such activities. As parents, grandparents or just friends, our job is to role model such behaviour. He needs to see that grownups can still play, be spontaneous, be creative, have imaginations, etc. By role modelling such behaviour we encourage him to remain playful for as long as possible. We are all aware our young girls are increasingly becoming sexualized at a very early age. They seek to wear makeup and 'adult' clothing, have a mobile phone, are interested in boys. This is actively encouraged by the world of 'grownups' – their parents, TV, advertising, the media - they are having such behaviour role-modelled to them. They are only following our lead. Children's play will always reflect the world around them. Listening in to young children playing is always a very useful tool in getting to know what the parents think! The way in which the parents interact with their children will influence their interaction when they become teenagers. This simple truth seems to be ignored and not recognized at present.

Quality time together

To provide a wide range of consumer goods, latest devices, games and up-to-date clothing is not to parent. There are no substitutes for spending quality time together. Driving them to clubs, groups and events seems to be the most common joint time nowadays, with the child listening on headphones in the back of the car. This isn't quality time. If the parents allow this to be the norm, then the consequences for them when these children become teenagers can become painful, damaging and difficult. Many 'difficult' teenagers I work with have trouble communicating with their parents. Almost invariably, I have to address the way in which the parents communicate first. The parents have not encouraged quality time together. They often give the impression they are resentful of the imposition on their lifestyle that has come with parenthood. Frequently, the role modelling the teenager has experienced as a child is one of arguments, silences, brooding and poor communication (and that's just the parents). The teenager learns the norm in his family is to be silent and non-communicative, and then to burst into aggressive confrontation. The parents become aggravated by the teenagers' reticence to speak, and bad language. A cycle of non-communication has been born.

Time and listening

Parents need to incorporate, from an early age, times and days when the family interacts as a whole, times when everyone plays games not costing lots of money, when there are shared laughter and tears. Evenings when the TV is off and the family shares time together. The parents must role model this, and that means ensuring it happens on a regular basis. You need to be imaginative, creative and challenging in the ways in which you do this. I recently published a book about rites of passage for boys, and someone phoned me up to tell me what they had done that had been inspired by the book. As parents of a 7-year-old boy who wet the bed at night, they decided they would jointly create a rite of passage for him, as he was equally frustrated by the behaviour. They agreed a series of tasks for him to achieve. He was to ride his bike to woodlands he liked being in, but had never visited alone before. Once there, he would sit on his own in the trees, and observe nature, see what was around, for several hours, without food. He'd ask for help from nature. Then he would select a stick, which he'd bring home, and he'd spend the evening whittling it. He'd always wanted to whittle but his parents had not allowed him. The family and the boy planned, discussed and arranged the event, which he felt was very challenging and tough. He succeeded, he brought home his stick and he spent the evening whittling. That night he didn't wet the bed, and he no longer does. He moved on, and his family supported him. It was achieved through discussion, mediation, spending quality time together and being imaginative.

Opportunities

Time, space and opportunities often restrict our participation with our children. Knowing that it is difficult, we still should attempt to offer some of the following, without beating ourselves up if we don't succeed:

*   *Provide opportunities for active play.*

*   *Throwing at targets, running, jumping rope, tumbling and aerobics may be of interest. These lead to team sports and the development of physical skills.*

*   *Provide opportunities to develop an understanding of rules by playing simple table games: cards, dominoes, tic-tac-toe, etc*

*   *Provide opportunities for children to do non-competitive team activities such as working a jigsaw puzzle or planting a garden.*

*   *Encourage children's sense of accomplishment, providing opportunities to build models, cook, crafts, practice music or work with wood.*

*   *All children like to follow older people, especially when they are 'doing' something. This is participation; they learn by watching.*

*   *Encourage children's collections by allowing them to make special boxes or books in which to store their collections.*

*   *Encourage reading and writing by allowing children to produce stories with scripts, create music for plays and puppet shows, produce a newspaper, record events, go on field trips or conduct experiments.*

*   *Help children explore their world by taking trips to museums, work places and other neighbourhoods.*

*   *Create time and space for the whole family to talk together and discuss issues and problems openly and with mutual respect.*

We are all responsible for children

There is an African saying, 'The child is brought up by the village.' This very important message has differing layers of meaning:

A child needs a variety of influences and role models, not just his parents.

The job of bringing up a child is far too important to allow just the parents to do it.

Every person is responsible for every child they come into contact with.

The children are the future of your community; it is essential that you take care of them.

Children are valuable and very important.

As parents we need to remember that we need support and help from others whilst bringing up our children; we can't do it all on our own. It's a very big task. Ask for help with the above list of activities.

THE AGE
Child

The baby is held by and is in very close contact with a limited number of people. When the baby becomes a child he starts to crawl, walk and run, and he encounters the wider community. Beyond his home for the first time he comes across people from outside his own immediate family. He is free to explore beyond the confines of hearth and home, and he willingly takes this opportunity. However, he always returns to his home. He still relies on his parents to feed him and keep him warm. The child plays, explores and is imaginative. He touches, feels, tastes, sees, hears the world for the first time. The connections between sound, taste, feel, and vocabulary become clear. In his exploration of the world he experiences awe and wonder. Awe can be positive and negative. We can be in awe of something which frightens us. The sheer size and scale of a tall cliff can attract us, but it can also be a little frightening. When I first came close to a large wild elephant, I was in awe, I was fascinated, but also very aware of his immense power, which was unsettling. To experience awe is always a personal but very immediate sensation. Awe engenders immediacy: we are no longer in a reverie, we become present. Such experiences are learning tools. When we feel wonder, we learn about the world, and we take in the messages being sent to us. The child is innocent, and is able to explore the world without preconception. Not to pre-judge our lives is one of the aims of all great spiritual teachings. To be in awe of the world enables us to learn and to grow. The innocent can encounter pleasure in a non-sexual way. Pleasure and stimulation are vital to growth and well-being.

To make definitive statements about where a child should be in terms of his development is very dangerous and can lead to problems. Each one of us needs to be allowed to develop at our own pace. However, there are certain broad developmental stages that can be outlined.

Pre-school
He is now interested in interacting with other people, so he is developing language and social skills. These skills are at this point focused very much on himself, his surroundings and the immediate close contacts he has.

Early school
The transition from pre-school to early school can be traumatic, but in most cases the child is eased in by the use of creativity, play and games. These help to slowly lessen his dependence on his prime carer. At this stage in development, he starts to expand his vocabulary and is able to share and to play with others in a constructive and deliberate way. Here he is still likely to confuse fantasy and reality at times; he should still be naïve, and he doesn't use adult logic. At about 4 or 5 he starts to distinguish between right and wrong, and understand the concept of honesty.

Middle school
It is widely recognized that children learn by playing and having fun, and by doing so they experiment and are able to develop dexterity and

language skills. Our present educational system decides that the child is ready to learn in a 'grown up' way from about age 7 onwards. I find this very difficult to understand. Instead of children continually learning through fun and play, they start to have to undertake exams. This change can be very difficult for children to manage as it can seem very judgmental. Suddenly they are being tested and measured against each other.

It is impossible to judge how 'advanced' or not a child is. I refused to learn how to read or write until I was about 8 or 9 years old. I did this mainly because I didn't like my teacher, particularly the way in which she forced us to read and write. I can remember her look of contempt for me, and the frequent visits to the headmaster for canings as my reluctance did little to warm our relationship. I wonder what she would think of me now earning my living by writing books and running creative writing classes!

THE PAST

When our more recent ancestors examined the ages, they called this stage 'Youth', and created some interesting ideas around the age. In the Renaissance this age was represented by the name *vita voluptatis* (the life of pleasure), as opposed to the *vita activa* (the life of action). The age was typically depicted as young men frolicking in fields! This frolicking was undertaken in a non-sexual, pre-pubescent way. It is a time of innocence and adventure, connecting to what Freud called the 'Pleasure Principle'. The child spends time amongst the flowers, the fields and pastures in innocent reverie. In a sense this age represented a utopian ideal. It needed to be explored and enjoyed while it lasted, but all too soon, other imperatives and motivations imposed themselves.

The Edwardian and Victorian principles applied to children changed rather dramatically, probably influenced by the increase in size of towns and cities. You needed to 'bring up' your children, and the conceits around the importance and significance of children changed. Here we developed a new way of interacting with our kids, summed up by the miserable saying 'children should be seen but not heard.' In the course of several hundred years we moved from the child being very important in rural families to being an inconvenience for the parent, and needing to 'grow up' as quickly as possible. There is a Jesuit maxim, 'Give me a child until he is seven, and I will show you the man.' Unfortunately we seemed to have misinterpreted this and we only allowed our offspring to be children until the age of 7, expecting them to grow up immediately after. In the Victorian era it was straight into employment at this age or earlier!

THE PRESENT

A lot of my working life has been spent with children who have been damaged, abused or have had to grow up too soon, many becoming carers for their parents at a very early age. I attempt to reconnect these children to the child within. We do this through play, creativity, laughter and the expression of wonder. When they understand it is safe to be childish, it is a great release for them. As soon as they start to play, I can see a huge weight lifted from their shoulders, and for seconds or minutes they are lost, consumed in wonder and joy. A great deal of my work with them relies on me being the positive role model. So, I may bring a large bag of wooden bricks and start making a house with them. If the individual still finds this too 'childish', then I tell a positive true story. These are the bricks I use when I work for major corporations and companies. I allow chief executives and managing directors to play with these, and they find it very helpful. The reticence of both children and adults soon disappears when they realize there is no judgement, no right or wrong, and they inevitably end up happily playing alongside me. The cumulative effect of allowing this back into our lives can be hugely influential and healing.

Growing up fast

In our society we are encouraged to grow up fast, we feel being childish or playing is frivolous or a waste of time, taking us away from the serious matters in our lives. The catalytic work I do with children and adults has always shown me that I need to retain my playfulness and be in wonder every day. This is not a call for a return to the 'dark ages' – no televisions, no technology, no sweets. We cannot ignore the fact that technology and the world has changed. It is how intrusive we allow it to become, and the quality and nurturing nature of the alternatives we offer, which is vital. The age of the child is about innocence. We should seek to preserve the innocence in the child for as long as possible. At some point he will be disappointed, he will be disillusioned. However, the longer he remains held in wonder the better. In order to do this the parents need to protect him, not overly, and not by using fear or intimidation. It is a very difficult and delicate balancing act. We need to be actively involved in their lives without smothering them. We need to encourage them out into the world without filling them with fear. Mothers and fathers have a very difficult job, and this balancing act changes and develops in complexity as the boy grows older.

Young dads and play

My work has also focused on developing the role of the father, and all too often dads don't play enough with their children. Many of the young fathers I work with have never played in their lives. One was a heroin addict who had weaned himself off the drug through the influence of his young daughter. His unhappy childhood had not included joy, play or creativity. As a young father and victim of domestic violence he was forced to take charge of his daughter, and it was the making of him. He spent hours drawing with her, and commented how he had never been encouraged to draw before, but how his daughter had always enjoyed his illustrations, so with her encouragements he persisted. By playing with and learning from his wonderfully imaginative and very intelligent daughter, he developed his own style of parenting. The two of them loved reading books together, and he created a rap style of reading children's stories at night-time, to which she very happily fell asleep.

It is a terrible state of affairs when dads feel intimidated and unable to play with their children. Many think it's the mother's domain, a bitter old remnant from our chauvinist past. I would like to think we have progressed from these ways of being, but it is only through discussion and encouragement that change will come about. An important part of being a father is to be a role model. Play with a man is different from play with a woman. I know this may offend some women, but it just is true. There is no value judgment being made in the statement – men don't play better, on the whole they play differently, and that is the importance. A man will tend towards more rough and tumble and his play may be more risk taking. Men tend to teach by doing rather than talking about it. They have a tendency to just start 'making, doing, playing, exploring', without talking about what they are doing beforehand. This makes the play different. One single mother I worked with was a teacher by profession and we discussed this particular way of playing. We discussed how she had always explained and carefully prepared play activities, set time aside in a clearly defined room, and the child given due notice. With my encouragement she went back home, straight into the child's room and started an imaginative playtime without explanation, expectation or pre-determined goal. She said it lasted for about 30 minutes, the whole house was turned upside down and she and her son laughed and cried together. They had the best of times. They both felt hugely moved by the experience, and now her son encourages her and actively seeks such play.

A child needs to be able to play, explore and be in wonder with women and with men. Without a good mix of the two, he will grow up lop-sided, without completion and wholeness, always seeking something he is not sure about. We have a great many such lop-sided young men and they all need to be encouraged to find the balance in themselves, in terms of their masculine and feminine side. Many have rejected their feminine side and express their disquiet through violence and aggression. Men can and should show boys how to be at ease with the feminine, and so can women. I am not saying only a man can stimulate the masculine or feminine in a boy, because women can do this job just as well, but let us encourage our men to explore this with their children. All too often boys and girls do not gain sufficient exposure to their fathers or to positive male role models, and this causes severe deficiencies in later life. Young men need to spend time in the company of older men as well. I'll discuss this in more depth later.

THE FUTURE

Part of becoming a child is encompassed in the concept of separation. The child, once he has been through his 'first footing' ceremony, separates from his carer and explores the wider world. In that moment he becomes the responsibility of the wider community. Until that moment he was the responsibility of the person who happened to be carrying him. So there is a change occurring and for the first time the child needs to play on his own. This can be a very painful time for the mother or primary carer, but it is essential for the wholesome development of the eventual human being. The child starts to amuse himself, and to develop games or experiences that occur not only on the physical but on the mental level. The imaginative play that now develops is his, and his alone – he personalizes his experience. This is mitigated against when he relies on technology to amuse himself. PlayStation, Game Boy, Wii and such do the work for him. They are for the convenience of the parent, not the child. These are a throwback to the Victorian ideal of *seen and not heard*. A reliance on technology at a young age deprives the child of personalized imaginative play, and this affects his later ability to make decisions, to be self-determining and to challenge the world. He will tend towards negativity rather than positivity.

Learning through play

In summation, children and their parents should be encouraged to play imaginatively and creatively as long as possible, both together and on their own. By playing they express and are in contact with awe and wonder, and these are vital learning tools. We all acknowledge that the best way to learn is through play, and we encourage this in our children until the age of about 6 or 7. Suddenly, they are taught in a different way, and this is not correct. We need to extend play and imaginative education for much longer in order for our children to learn more completely about the world. Our education system reflects our own imbalances and emotional inadequacies as a society, and we impose them on our children at an early age.

The innocence of childhood is a wonderful thing, but all too soon changes occur in the child, which means they are ready to move onto the next age. The loss of innocence is to be grieved, but for the child, there is an inevitability and urgency in his wish to move on to the next age. Driven biologically and hormonally he leaves his play and exploration time and steps towards the next age, his teenage years.

SUGGESTIONS FOR ACTION
Imaginative play

Imaginative play, the creation of fantasy, and the development of an understanding of fun, joy and love are all related and essential for our development. By participating in these types of activities, children are learning about themselves and the wider world. They are putting into context the experiences they gather, and this affects their understanding of what is reality. As young children they find it difficult to understand the difference between reality and fantasy; indeed, most of the time there are both present. My very young son would play hide and seek. He'd hide behind the curtains, secure in the knowledge that no one could see him. In reality, the curtains didn't reach the floor, so his legs were clearly visible to us. At a certain point he put two and two together and realized we could see him. As fully developed human beings we need to know the difference between fantasy and reality most of the time. As young children we don't! We retain this ability to mix reality and fantasy until we are about 7 or even older. It is a wonderful state to be in, it really defines what it is to be 'childish' and I'm all in favour of returning there as adults as well.

Children need to be able to play and be imaginative by themselves. This is how they learn. It helps them to start to understand the complex nature of reality. I believe early exposure to cyberspace and too much television will affect a child's understanding and appreciation of fantasy. Many of the children I work with are exposed to cyberspace and television for long hours in a day. This prevents them from actively exploring and developing their spatial awareness. In other words, they are either lying down or sitting as they explore three-dimensional games. This can be confusing to the brain and the body. A young child needs to actually physically explore reality in order to be able to fully understand it. We do not experience the world only through our mind and eyes. As young children we need to interact with all our senses.

Cyberspace

As parents, my wife and I didn't allow our children a television or computer in their room. They could only use the ones in our living room. Our children are not horribly damaged by the experience, and don't feel they were deprived (although at times they certainly objected). They are both very competent with modern technology and computers. By not being able to secrete themselves away whilst interacting with cyberspace, our children were able to experience a continuum of awareness – from fantasy and imaginative play to development of self, development of spatial awareness, exploration of physical reality, understanding of what is solid, etc. I am not against all of the games and the imaginative aspects of cyberspace. I believe they can serve a very good purpose in the development of our children's imaginations and creativity. I know that children will be able to understand and use cyberspace correctly once they have explored physical reality completely themselves. The children of the future need to be encouraged to play and be imaginative without cyberspace for their early years, then introduced to it slowly, and with care. A sharing of the experience is good. The development of family games through Wii seems to be a very sensible growth. This enables the parents to role model use, length of time on the equipment and the play aspects.

Unfortunately, a great many parents are neglecting their parental responsibilities to role model and develop imaginative play with their children and relying on television and gaming as a distraction for long periods of time. In most offices and work places, there is an implicit understanding of the importance of breaks and time out whilst working in front of computer screens. Staff are encouraged to take breaks every hour or so. Yet parents are not applying this to their children. Many children, at a very young age, are sat in front of computer screens for up to ten or twelve hours a day. This is child neglect.

9

Rite of passage
Bravery

The Lesson
Questioning

The Age
Teenager

South

The colour of **Red**
Vigour and strength

THE FOURTH AGE
Teenager

THE RITE OF PASSAGE
Bravery

This particular rite of passage is a crucial one in determining the future balance and well-being of the adult to come. The boy needs to separate from his parents, start to understand his own unique nature and make his way in the world, he is seeking to become a man. All of these changes are scary, and he will need to be brave to achieve them. He needs to do the following work:

Separation - *The boy separates from his mother (and father)*
Transition - *He moves out of the home and seeks to define himself*
Incorporation - *He connects with his peers and with elders*

I was fortunate enough to work with First Nations teachers, and during my time with them, I undertook a series of shamanic journeys to meet spirit guides who could help me. These guides offered assistance and stories connecting back through the ages. The process involved entering a trance state, and then consciously bringing back the message. Here is one of those messages:

Grandfather Pipe Carrier

I was on the earth, I walked this life, I know who you are and how you are.
I was a baby, a child and then a teenager.
When I was a teenager, I rejected my society, I rebelled.
I was wild, I went insane, I needed to do this.
I became brave, I went to live in the wilderness,
I contemplated wildness. I felt hurt.
In that state, I was in pain.
I knew my wounds and I saw their worth and value.
By accepting pain I was able to transform it into love.
I transformed my pain into love by understanding how to go with the flow,
by crossing the threshold.
I went deep into the earth, with my pain, not leaving it on the surface.
The pain came with me,
and by going deep into the earth I was able to cross into another state.
A state of grace, acceptance and serenity.
All men need to do this, they need to plunge into the earth, wholeheartedly,
and accept the consequences of their actions,
then come back to become of value to their society.

For me this sums up the teenage journey. There is bravery and a stepping beyond boundaries. There is also self-examination, contemplation. Often there is a good deal of pain, angst, frustration. By facing up to these feelings, by stepping into them, we can come out the other side as a new person, a man. It is a typical rite of passage from confusion through pain to understanding. This year I started on a new programme for late teens and early twenties to develop skills and find themselves. The fundamental work programme hasn't changed since 1975 when I first started. This transformative process is and always has been the same for all of us. Yet, each time I do this work, it is subtly different, because each individual brings their own issues, their own take on reality, and that is why I still love being with teenagers, after all these years. It is impossible to say here what each boy needs in order for him to become a man, but as I said earlier, there is a communality in the experience. A rite of passage from boyhood into manhood is a long and difficult process. I would be foolish to say there is only one way you can do it, so I won't. However, in this chapter I will discuss the key elements of the rite, and the bare minimum of understanding we need to bring to the situation. I have called the rite of passage 'bravery', linking it to the concept of the First Nations people of America in terms of their young braves. I far prefer the name brave to warrior – braves can be vulnerable and tender as well as ferocious, whereas warriors are associated with war.

When we talk of rites of passage this is the rite we are most familiar with, and yet it is the rite we tend to do badly. Culturally, we seem to leave our boys to become men on their own, without support, which causes many problems. This is the one rite which needs the most care and attention. In a sense this time is pivotal and can make or break the future man; most other rites are either natural or gentler. This rite needs to accommodate three massive changes – the boy moves out of his home, he finds his friends and allies, he seeks his destiny. If we enable the boy to do this work well, it will set him up for the rest of his life. If we don't, the boy will struggle thereafter. I can't even start to describe the complexity and depth needed here. Suffice to say I have written a book on the subject, *Using The Ugly Duckling to find the Missing Link between Boys and Men*. In that book I talk about the multiplicity of effects which this rite of passage have on a boy and his community, and I think it is useful to describe some of those layers here.

The boy has to break free from the ties binding him to his immediate family.
This family has been his complete world. It has supported and sustained him. It has provided home, security, nourishment, education and warmth.

These ties are strong and have been in place for many years. In order to break free from them he has to push with a lot of strength and determination. A wise teacher told me that the boy who stays at home and never cuts the ties lives in a world of anger, blaming people for his inability to achieve in life, whereas the boy who leaves home and cuts the ties lives in a world of guilt, guilty for breaking away and leaving people behind. It's a tough choice, but for me the teenager must break free.

The teenager is like a little bird within the egg. He has grown from a naked chick, he has started to grow feathers yet he remains within the egg, and now he grows a beak, a hard beak. The sharpness and harshness of this beak is essential, if it isn't hard, it is of no use. He uses the beak intuitively to break open the shell and to liberate himself. If he doesn't break the shell he will die, he will suffocate confined within the eggshell. He shatters the egg in order to live. At the point of liberation from the shell he looks back and sees the broken remnants of the shell, the shell which has protected him thus far in his life. He feels guilty as he sees the shell will never be the same again. **After a teaching by Martin Prechtel.**

The beak represents 'attitude'. The teenager has to adopt attitude in order to be able to move on and away from his home. Previously, he has accepted and gone along with everything the family has decided to do. Now, crucially, he has to start making those decisions for himself, and he starts to question when and why those decisions are being made. By doing so he becomes self-centred, that is, he focuses more on his own needs rather than the collective needs of the family. This is all natural, positive and to be expected. Such a shift should not come as a surprise – it has happened for hundreds of thousands of years. The gravitational pull connecting him to his family is very strong. In order to break away he has to exert a strong force in the opposite direction. Only by adopting attitude can he effect this change.

The boy needs to break the ties binding him to his mother
This sounds harsh, but it is absolutely necessary. It doesn't mean he stops loving his mother. It doesn't mean he rejects his mother. It means he needs to find support and encouragement from outside his family, away from his mother. He can do this work better by finding the company of other men. Please read *Iron John* by Robert Bly, if you want the significance and detail of this important part of the rite explained. The mother has cared and looked after him until this point, but she is now unable to help him. Indeed, if she tries to do this work it will confuse and disorientate him. There is a huge amount of grief around this rite of passage and the mother crucially needs support from elders, as well as the boy, during this transition. Indeed, the father needs such support as well, because he, again, can't do the work. He may be able to assist in small ways, but he too needs to stand aside and let his son move on, out into the world. Within the child a transformation occurs. He increases his testosterone, grows hairy and his voice changes. Many things happen which baffle and confuse him and his parents. He actually starts to smell differently, and if some scientific studies are to be believed, this new smell repels his parents.

Defining himself

The teenagers are seeking to define themselves anew, not as the sons of their mothers, but as individuals. The creation of a new, original identity is vital. This new person is best created by following a calling – finding what they are good at – rather than trying to conform to other people's ideas of who they are. The expectations of parents and teachers need to be challenged (attitude again). Most parents have conditional and preconceived ideas about what their children should be doing with their lives. My mother wanted me to be a doctor. Fortunately, I was able to resist my mother's desires very easily as I didn't gain the necessary qualifications. Such external desires and wishes are not always useful for teenagers, and if they are pursued, they can lead to very unhappy adults who feel trapped and as though there is something missing from their lives.

The teenager is on a quest to find his own soul's purpose and he needs to follow his intuition. There are ways of knowing when he is in the right place – the job which comes naturally and with ease, the work which makes him happy, the friends with whom he is at ease, those moments he feels enlivened, enthusiastic and energized. He is seeking the reason he was born, connecting himself to his unique skill, his abilities, personality and gifts. It is actually very simple to find the soul's purpose – you just follow your joy. He needs to know what makes him happy, and then find ways to share this with the wider community.

When I was a teenager I drifted. I was sacked from jobs. I didn't find much satisfaction in work. Living on the dole with little prospect of employment in 1981 forced me to reappraise my life. I decided I wanted to combine the two things making me happy – creating art and working with children. Such jobs weren't being advertised in the Job Centre, so I set about becoming them myself. After about five or six years, I had a stable business that provided employment for both myself and a large number of others. Despite people's belief that creating such work would be difficult, I actually found it very simple. I was very determined and prepared to work long hours, but I knew I could do it. I defined myself, and I followed my soul's purpose. This is vital work, as it will influence how we interact with the world throughout the rest of our life. Those who have found their soul's purpose will be happy, joyous, strong and of service to others. Those who haven't found it will tend to be unhappy, angry, confused, selfish and cynical about life. We have a great many people out there who have not found their soul's purpose. The teenager's peers can help him on this journey. They can encourage him, test him and push him to find out about himself. Together they can form alliances, they can fight enemies, they can bond, they can build empires.

Peer pressure and support is positive; it will enable him to understand his place in the pecking order.

Pecking order

During this age we test each other out. The flexing of muscles, both physical and metaphorical, is expected. It enables the teenagers to build their friendship and work circles. This inevitably leads to rivalries, disappointments, misunderstandings and trouble, as well as bonding, friendships and love. The development of a pecking order is completely normal, but when it is operating in the negative it can lead to bullying, violence and despair. When it is operating in the positive it leads to non-violent resolutions, collaboration, harmony and community. Most teenage pecking orders are based on fairly simple and superficial judgments. In the early 1970s I worked with teenagers in a children's home. In the home they were very confident. Entering the outside world, some became subservient and meek. I realized it was about their clothing and image, the kids wore second-hand clothes and were very conscious of it. When they were out in the city and confronted by kids wearing new and better clothing, they instantly assumed their place in the pecking order. Of course as adults we don't do such a thing... Oh yes we do! We manipulate and use pecking orders throughout our lives. Decisions are made consciously and unconsciously all the time. Who do you sit next to? Who do you speak to at the party? Judgments and prejudice exist in us all.

Paradoxically, as teenagers define themselves they have a strong drive to conform. Classically, the Goth teenager says to his parents he is just expressing his individuality by dressing this way, and then dismisses anyone not wearing Goth clothes. In doing so, they form strong peer alliances and bonds, which are very useful in later life. They are creating the communities of the future. All genres of music can create these niches into which the young people can climb – hip hop, grime, drum and bass – they are alliances made to create identity, our unique stamp on the world. To do all these things and to take flight away from home in a constructive, positive, manner requires courage, and will take many years.

THE LESSON
Questioning

Teenagers need to ask the very important question 'Why?' Their task is to question everything, and this is a very important social stage. In a child's eye his parents have always been correct. A teenager challenges this, and we must take the time and effort to explain things for him. Our answers cannot be the glib ones suitable for young children; we must answer them as adults. Often when they question culture and society and their infrastructures, they highlight inadequacies and faults in them that we need to address. They are inquisitive and intelligent, and may well bring a new perspective to old problems. Teenagers are the break in the chain. They do this out of love and respect. They are vital to the overall progress of humanity, as they stimulate progress. They also define themselves with their questioning. They are stating an opinion, and this opinion may be different from that of the parents. We need to carry this inquisitive and free-spirited nature into our later lives. We need to retain the 'rebel' in all of us, the one who stands outside and looks in, without falling into the trap of just objecting for the sake of it. There needs to be an intelligence to such behaviour.

Shared parenting

Parents know how teenagers are very adept at dividing people and seeking out weaknesses and differences. Blackmail, emotional and monetary, devious lying – all are fair tools in the business of gaining advantages and favours ('But mum said I can stay out until 11'). Ideally, the parents of the teenager need to collaborate, and both agree on the script and the boundaries. An equality of decisions, responsibility, and being the good or bad cop is essential. Good luck with all that! However, to focus on the negative is not useful. The parents of a teenager can have a great deal more freedom. They have an adult in the making on their hands – such a blessing. There came a point with my two children when our conversations changed. I asked them for advice and help, I shared my own past, my own pain. I trusted them to be able to receive and give within our relationship, and it has been a blessing for me in so many ways. I feel very privileged to know, and to be friends with, my own children. They have grown into very intelligent and sensible human beings (with such clever parents they didn't have a choice!)

Convenience parenting

As we are encouraged to focus more and more on work and our career, we are becoming more formulaic and less involved in our parenting of children. Busy with work, parents do not spend time with their children; they employ other people to do it. This means the children don't really know their parents, and the parents don't really know their children. Part of this cycle has created what I call 'convenience parenting'. The encumbrance of having to bring up a child or children is minimized by our reliance and dependence on artefacts, people and services – for the benefit of the parent, not the child. From birth onwards the needs of the child are subservient to the wants of the parents, and this can be damaging for the developing child. I am increasingly being asked to work with troubled families where the parents have not really spent 'quality' time with their children. They have relied on nannies, nurseries, television, the internet and schoolteachers to care for, educate and nurture their children. As problems arise the parents blame these other agents for the bad behaviour of their children. They refuse to see their own lack of involvement as being often crucial to the behaviour.

Becoming parents alters and affects our social life. It takes some people a great deal of time to realize that they have responsibilities and commitments as a parent. I have to introduce some of the parents to the idea that spending time with their children can be fun, of benefit and actually healing for them. They have spent so little time with their children that they need to be 'taught' how to interact with them, or even how to have fun with them. As discussed in the last chapter, when we renege on our time with our children it will almost invariably come back to haunt us with our teenagers.

The rage of a teenager

When a convenience parent is suddenly confronted by a raging, scary teenager who seems to have appeared from nowhere there is a great deal of shock and surprise. The teenager has often been so side-lined, suppressed, ignored, disenfranchised, rebutted and farmed out that he has a great deal of rage, and is now prepared to kick and shout in order to be seen and heard. Many younger children attempt to conform, be quiet and be good during their formative years. This strategy comes from their wish to please their parents. All they've wanted in return is to be listened to, and receive attention. By the time they become teenagers they realize this strategy has failed. They haven't received the attention, love and care they wanted by being 'good'. So what alternative is open to them? Gain the attention by other means. Too many parents of teenagers come to me and say, 'I can't understand it, I gave him everything he wanted.' But material goods mean nothing; without love, time and personal attention they are hollow. These parents then add, 'I just want him to be good, well behaved, not use drugs, not to get the girl pregnant.' If he does all this, it would simply be more convenient for the parents.

84

Kevin and Perry

The brilliant comedy sketches of 'Kevin and Perry', as enacted by Harry Enfield and Paul Whitehouse, illustrated the intransigence and confusion of these times – the teenagers not communicating, and the parents bravely trying to keep the channels open. The sketches showed accurately the misunderstandings and different interpretations that occur at this time. These problems are not just from our modern times, however. They have occurred the world over for many thousands of years. The parents need to remember teenagehood is just a phase, although how long it will last is anyone's guess! This is the phenomenon every parent dreads – the teenager becoming monosyllabic, withdrawn and argumentative. It often comes about because the teenager lacks the confidence to express his thoughts or opinions, and lacks the drive or motivation to find or define himself. Suffice to say, if as parents you have already instilled some dialogue, play and sense of creativity in your relationship, this will now pay dividends as it will prevent them from shutting down completely.

Boundaries and accepting responsibility

My work with many families is to resurrect or create anew a family sense of humour and justice. Often the parents interpret the behaviour of the boy as confrontational when it is actually just an expression of confusion. The teenagers can be pushing boundaries at some times, but are reassured by them at others. With one family the parents dictated the boy should be home by 10:30 and it became a very important battleground. Through discussion we were able to come to a compromise of 11:30 being seen as reasonable. Both sides had backed down, the parents from 10:30, the boy from 1:00am. The boy accepted he was being unrealistic about the time for return. In subsequent conversations with the boy on his own, he actually appreciated coming home at that time, as it meant he didn't stay out with the rougher and more unruly kids. He admitted he had felt tired and ill at ease on the streets that late at night, although he would never admit this to his parents. He was still able to blame his parents for his return to home, but wasn't seen as a complete wimp by his peers. He took on the responsibility of returning home at the appointed hour, and he returned at 11:30. As a consequence the parents didn't wait up for the boy the next weekend, they didn't have a fight and in the morning they brought the boy his breakfast in bed, and he did the washing up. Sense, trust and responsibility had returned to the family.

Rites of passage for parents and teenager

Paradoxically, it is often the parents who are not doing sufficient to encourage the teenagers out into the world. To leave home we need to be brave, and it is a balancing act between wanting to leave our childhood behind and starting as a grown up. The parents need help and assistance with this task, just as much as the teenagers do. In a sense this rite of passage is not just about the teenager accepting the challenge of separation, but it is just as relevant for the parents. They have to be heroic too, and allow the boy to become a man. Many parents feel afraid for their child and don't want him to 'get hurt' out there. We seem to have forgotten quite how complex this work is. We expect our teenagers to complete the process in a few months, a year at the most, and then everything can return to being 'normal' again. The whole point is that, as parents of teenagers, your lives will never be the same again – there is no going back. Parenting was never about convenience or simplicity. When we held that tiny baby in our arms we never thought about the teenager lying dormant in him, we just wanted a simple life.

THE AGE
Teenager
Transition to Teen Time
The preteen period is a mixture of emotions, changes and paradoxes.

These can include the following:

* *They want to be taken seriously, but they can also still behave very selfishly and childishly.*
* *They want to be thought of as 'cool', but may also still like his fluffy toys.*
* *Boys like to feel big and act tough with their mates, but they are very scared underneath.*
* *Girls interest and fascinate him, but they also intimidate and scare.*
* *The friendship and closeness of his girlfriend is more important than anything else in the world, until they break up the following week, and he finds someone else.*

The preteen can be very self-centred. He may not be very socially aware or adept. He may frustrate his parents with his mood swings and changes of mind, but this is only the precursor to his move into full-blown teenagehood.

Hold on, it may be a bumpy ride!

There is a huge difference between a 13 year old and a 19 year old. You need to treat them differently. In a sense calling them teenagers is wrong, as the process and changes they are involved in can take many years to resolve, often 15 years or longer. They are making a transition from being a child to being a grown up, and this is not simple. They are seeking to become initiated; they want to pass through a rite of passage to manhood; they want to be accepted as grown-ups. It would be more realistic to say '18 to 30-hood'.

Testosterone

During his teenage years the boy changes physically and this is mostly down to testosterone, a hormone found in both men and women. Not a great deal is known about testosterone, but it is blamed for many things, and I think it is badly misunderstood. The effects of an increase in testosterone can vary hugely between individuals and differ at different times in people's lives. For me the association of testosterone with violence and war is cultural rather than physiological. As W. Cannon said in his book *Bodily Changes in Pain, Hunger, Fear and Rage,* 'testosterone is truly associated with adrenaline and the flight or fight response.'[*4] My experiences lead me to agree.

Evolutionary theory

To explain this we need to remember the history lesson we were taught in our early gestation. We need to know that we were once a fish, then a bird, before finally becoming a mammal. Each one grew naturally from the other and mutually supported each other in its development; they didn't compete. Darwin laid out certain ground rules in evolutionary competence, and we have confused these by adopting the phrase 'survival of the fittest', which didn't appear in the first editions of *The Origin of Species.* When a species is adept at flight it increases its chances of surviving and overcoming the vagaries of weather, climate, geography, topography, natural predators, other species in competition and fellow members of its own species. This essential skill is in the recognizing of the percentages and advantages of choosing one or the other option:

Fight	*Flight*
take arms	run away
violence	non-violence
stand up to a challenge	compromise
individualism	mutual support
short term	long term

For over 90% of the time, the flight option is the optimum choice. The way of violence and fighting is very rarely viable or worthwhile. So almost invariably when the rush of testosterone or adrenaline comes, the choice is flight. Testosterone encourages us to make those choices correctly, and it is actually connected to our ability to mutually support and live collaboratively. So, when a boy increases his testosterone levels, through feeling fear he is actually increasing the likelihood of him taking flight rather than fighting. He isn't moving to becoming a violent yob; he's preparing to avoid conflict.

The representation of teens in the media

The changes needed can take years to come about. They often continue long into our twenties and thirties, and beyond! We are presently expecting our teenage boys to either do this work on their own, or amongst their peers. In our society we have almost outlawed our teenagers. Their exploration of the self and the boundaries of behaviour are seen as antisocial and intolerable. Many of our teenagers are expected to become men behind the local alcohol selling shop. The media reports with alacrity how young men are out of control – addiction, violence and depression hit the headlines. These young men are experiencing a maelstrom of emotions and reacting to them in a variety of ways. However, not all our teenagers are vandals and delinquents; indeed, only a very small percentage are. The demonization of 'hoodies' has enabled our young people to be easily compartmentalized as 'trouble-makers', when all they are doing is making a fashion statement. Similarly, in my youth, long hair on a man was a 'bad' thing, despite the fact that it was intended to show how peaceful and loving you were. The press and the media are able to work themselves into frenzies over very insignificant and unimportant matters, which handicap and hinder our young people. The teenagers are only doing what all previous generations have done and questioning the establishment.

Porn

Ideally our teenagers should be exploring the differences between sensuality and sexuality, and the delicious mix of emotions and feelings that they induce. However, a large number of our teenagers have never been introduced to the idea that sensuality is separate from sexuality.

Porn doesn't help this at all. Boys and men watch images of individuals mechanically and violently being sexual. By being exposed to this, they take in messages about what is sexual and how to behave if you want to be a man. Many young men I work with have 'porn star' at the top of their list of desirable jobs. The association with money, kudos and fame, together with the availability of 'pussy' seems to them to be ideal. When I ask about the need for relationships and friendship, they feel such things are irrelevant and encumbrances, saying 'I want to be free.' Yet, this freedom equates to the physical act, not the combination of mind, emotion, sensuality and sex. Porn stars are no longer viable porn stars if they let the mind or emotion in – they become, literally, flops. These boys see no place for sensuality, communication, emotion, pleasure or desire, just lust and physical gratification. This distorted view is supported and encouraged by their peers, and becomes their goal and wish. When they are then confronted by a real woman, who has emotions, wants love, has crooked breasts and is not always up for sex, they are disappointed. When I work with teenagers we are able to go beyond the tough front and exterior. There we really discuss intimate details and what really feel good, and almost invariably these young men remember the soft moments, the still pleasures, the stroking and caressing, as being restorative and pleasurable. There is hope.

If we can enable these young men to just take a few moments to reflect, to really look into their hearts, they all connect to the very basic human need – to be wanted, to be loved, to be desired and for it to be a two way process. This is the key – reminding them of the two-way nature of sensuality and sensuality, the push me–pull you of reciprocity and the pleasures that come from such intimacy. We have a great deal of work still to be done in this field, but I am always optimistic about the future. Young men have the chance to become emotionally intelligent, far more than previous generations. I'm sure the focus on porn is just a phase with the opening of the internet. Once that dissipates then it will fall back to a more enlightened and caring equilibrium.

Masturbation

Sensual awareness of being content and happy with oneself leads to sexuality at some point in time. The obvious first manifestation of this is masturbation. Masturbation can still be seen as taboo, unpleasant and distasteful, and this needs to be conquered. I can remember an R.E. lesson on sex education when I was 14. My friend Steve piped up with the question we all wanted answering: 'Is it true you go blind if you masturbate too much?' We waited with bated breath for the answer. 'No.' A communal sigh of relief from all the boys filled the room.

In order to be able to love others you need to love yourself first, and masturbation is the teenager's route to such a goal; indeed, it is probably needed throughout maturation. We need to practice before we share our sexuality with another. As Steve Biddulph says *'For men willing to utilize their imagination and capacities for fantasy, masturbation is an exercise in sexual independence and in practicing sensuousness. It needs to be – from the accounts of many women, the majority of men need all the practice they can get! By not rushing, by experimenting, we become more skilful and sensuous lovers. By having a playful and happy approach to self-pleasuring, men and their lovers benefit enormously.'*[5]

Sexuality through sensuality

In school young men are taught the mechanics of sex, and porn teaches them the visceral intensity of sexuality, but both are de-humanized, impersonal, and without meaning. If he doesn't receive the right messages from school and the internet, where will he find them? From his peers? Should parents be involved in the sex education of their children?

91

These are important questions, and I think there is an ideal progression in terms of open discussion at home, then amongst his peers and the wider world.

Sensuality at home

From an early age our boys need to be held and caressed by their parents. They must feel this is natural and acceptable. They must not feel that to be naked is somehow bad or wrong, and they should be comfortable about their own body shape and look. My father would always walk naked from his bath in the evening to his bedroom. This may seem ridiculous to some, but it reminded me that it is OK to be naked, even though as a teenager it caused me huge embarrassment. The teenager needs to feel able to experiment with self-pleasing and loving whilst in the privacy of his bedroom, not to be guilty and embarrassed by it. The parents need to express their awareness of it in a way that accepts it as natural.

Sexuality amongst his peers

He will discuss and learn from his peers. Many young teenagers learn the full facts of life from their mates, and we have to hope that they are receiving a caring, supportive and loving picture. He will be encouraged to experiment by his peers and may well learn some weird things. As parents we need to be open enough to encourage open and frank dialogue, though such discussions will never be easy. As a boy he could possibly experiment with other boys at this time, and this may be a phase or not. Allow him time to try things out without judgement.

Enlightened and advanced support from elders and the wider world

Questions need to be asked and if the teenager can find more experienced peers and older men who can discuss the issues frankly and openly, then he is behaving sensibly.

Starting sexual relationships

What the teenager needs to find within his exploration of the senses is the connection that leads him beyond sex and into making love. This comes through an understanding of the self, the connectedness of the self to another and through that union a connection to so much more – the impossible, the greatest potential, the cosmos itself. This level of intensity and expression relies heavily on the union being emotionally intelligent, on the man being able to communicate and on him knowing himself. He needs to know what he is capable of and to seek it sensibly and with joy.

To give advice on this matter or to say what such a relationship should be in a book such as this would be impossible. Each one of us knows how complex and delicate such things are. All I can say is that the finding of a partner to share your life with is one of the most beautiful things in the world, and it can also be very difficult! The development of the relationship needs to be the balancing of the male and the female, and the Yin and Yang symbol represents this perfectly – the male and female supporting and mutually assisting each other, the seed of the one being in the other. Teenagers can throw themselves into relationships; they can live, breath and be close to someone with an intensity and fervour which we may see as being idealistic or foolish. But, we must support them in these endeavours, they are the experiments we all need to have in order to find the right person. They are seeking to find a partner, someone to share their lives with, it is a natural progression for all human beings.

THE PAST

Our ancestors were very cognizant of this rite, both here in Europe and on every continent of the planet. They prepared for many years in order to accommodate this important time into their culture; indeed, it was recognized as part of their culture. There are examples to be found still in indigenous people from all over the planet as well as in ancient texts from Europe. Each society created and performed a different rite depending on the cultural needs and circumstances of the people. The number of boys needing initiation dictated whether it would occur once a year, or once in a cycle of years. In all of them the boys were set tasks and tested. The severity of the rite reflected the nature of the culture. In other words, the hunter-gatherers orientated the test to encourage hunter-gathering skills in the boys, whilst the agriculturalists honed different and more particular skills. There were similarities between all rites, and there is an identifiable core of intent within teenage rites from the past.

* Each boy was given a mentor who was an older man, not his father, who supervised and encouraged him through the test and beyond.

* The physical separation of the boy from the family needed to be ritualized and could be a complex and important part of the rite, even though he might actually only be living two hundred yards from his home.

* The boys moved from living amongst women to living solely with men.

* The boy's family was supported in their grief around the loss of the boy.

* The boys were given freedom to express themselves. This was expressed in how they dressed, how they behaved; individually they were encouraged to create an appearance or style. In return for this freedom the boys were given responsibilities and tasks by the community.

* No boy would undertake such a rite on his own. He underwent it amongst his peers.

* The rite took the form of a test for the boys, which they needed to pass in order to become a man. This was reflected in the cycle of 'initiate, initiation and completion'.

* The boys were encouraged to come through the test as a group. They needed to bond with each other; they needed to understand mutual support and collaboration.

* The tests were used to show individual expertise and skill.

* The solutions to the tests lay within the wisdom and knowledge of the mentors, and they had to impart and pass on this knowledge.

*   The boys were encouraged to understand that generations of men had undergone the tests in the same way. They realized that this was part of their ancestral inheritance.
*   The wider community was involved in preparing and developing specific tasks and tests for the rites of passage, and particularly in developing elaborate celebrations on graduation.

This list comes from my own extensive research and contact with indigenous peoples from around the world. It was difficult for me to comprehend how significant and important this rite was, and still can be, until I experienced it first-hand. I made a documentary film with a semi-nomadic tribe in the north of Kenya, the Samburu, about their boys' rite of passage, and the event had a profound effect on me. I was asked to make the film by a local charitable trust, as the elders recognized the ritual was fast dying out, and wanted a permanent record. Living with a semi-nomadic people for many months, being confronted by a totally foreign culture, and witnessing the un-anaesthetized circumcision of 106 boys all came as a shock.

Muratare – circumcision

The Samburu need to know their young men will defend their cattle and lands with bravery, so they circumcise the boys. The elders told me they needed to be able to look into their boys' eyes at the point of circumcision, see no fear and therefore know that they would defend their cattle. The Samburu carry spears and knives, but they are surrounded by tribes carrying AK47s, as well as living with elephants and lions. I do not agree with the ritual mutilation of the boys, but it was fascinating to see the commitment and dedication that came with it, and the ways in which it was used to create community. I fully support their right to do what they feel is correct in order to preserve their culture.

The young boys of the Samburu looked forward with great anticipation to their initiation into manhood by circumcision ritual (Muratare), which

95

occurs once every twenty or so years. The braves (L'murrani) – boys who have been circumcised, but who haven't married – are able live very freely. They spend a huge amount of time painting and adorning themselves, but are fearsomely protective of their tribal lands. To our outsider's eyes, they may look like dilettantes and posers, but they are being supervised in their teenagehood by elders. They are given the responsibility of looking after the cattle, which are essential to the wellbeing of the community and represent its wealth. Each family has goats and sheep which they take care of themselves, but the L'Murrani look after everyone's cattle as a whole. They will be punished severely if they lose cattle. They know the dire consequences to the whole community if the cattle are lost and will kill those who try to steal them. They are given clear boundaries even within their freedom.

Humiliation

During the act of circumcision in the Samburu, there is humiliation. The boys spend months being encouraged to be brash and openly aggressive; they strut and preen. Then at the moment of circumcision they are publicly humiliated. They are surrounded by literally hundreds of people, some of whom they know, others they don't. These are the spectators, come to witness the circumcision. The boy is firmly gripped by his elders; they forcibly control him. As the circumciser makes his way round the village, some boys quake uncontrollably and some literally leave their bodies, whilst others stand impassively like cows blankly observing the mounting crescendo of chaos around them. The moment arrives. They are brusquely stripped naked and water and milk are poured over the head. The shock of cold fluids pushes them down onto a spread cow skin. Their legs are spread wide. Everyone crowds in and gawps. Fights break out as people vie for the best views. There is no privacy – this is a very public display. For a people who never see each other naked, this is their darkest fear, a very frightening scene. There is no hiding. They are minutely observed from every angle, as the crowd looks for flinching or other displays of discomfort. This will bring dishonour onto their families; they will be banned from village life if their boys cry out or show discomfort. The boys are cut and bleed openly, and then they are wrapped in the cow skin and carried into their ceremonial bed, where they can moan and groan. The next day the boys are either in bed or walking gingerly around the village. Their faces have been transformed. No longer brash and cocky, they are humble and very quiet. They have been publicly exposed and cut down to size, and their humiliation is complete. They have submitted themselves to the laws of their people. They have sacrificed their dignity for the good of their ancestors and elders, and publicly committed themselves to their traditions and culture. They have demonstrated an ultimate act of respect – incomprehensible and alien to our Western mind-set.

At the graduation ceremony a month later, the elders and I sat facing Mount Kenya to offer our thanks to Spirit (N'Gai). Within those prayers we thanked all those who had helped us and guided us through difficult times. One elder offered thanks to N'gai for allowing all the boys to live through the ritual. For the Samburu it was quite remarkable that none of the boys had died, although one had come within ten minutes of losing his life, according to the doctors who saved him from bleeding to death after circumcision. As part of the boys' maturation they undertook arduous and dangerous treks into the wilderness; they had been forced to march huge distances without food and water, they had cut and burnt themselves in preparation for the pain and they had been humbled by the public circumcision in a remembrance of ancestral duty and responsibility. This process bonded them as a group, and toughened them to take the pain of circumcision. I witnessed probably the last time such a ritual will have been undertaken, and the bravery of those boys will stay with me forever. I do not suggest we should try to recreate such a brutal and dangerous ritual here in our civilized world. But the principles and long-term consequence of such a ritual is very much needed right now. To copy an ancient foreign ceremony like this would be absurd, but to ignore the need for such rites would also be negating our responsibility to the future generations.

Graduation

The boys graduate at the end of a long ritual, lasting up to six months, in this time the community had moved from their homes to a ceremonial village which the women had constructed. The families maintaining two homes for the duration which is a great strain on them. Once the boys become braves they are expected only to eat and drink with their fellow initiates; indeed, no brave is allowed to eat or drink alone. They must collaborate with each other wherever possible. This has been a major feature of all teenage rites of passage. The apprenticeships undertaken in the steel industry, for example, taught that all jobs were dangerous and you needed to be supported and work as a team. The coal industry was the same – when you go down a pit, you can't do the work on your own, so you must collaborate, work as a team. This showed the boys how to ask for help, how to share; not how be hard, but how to become flexible and responsive.

Bravery

These rituals stimulate bravery. Bravery comes rarely in our culture, but in indigenous cultures bravery it is expected and encouraged. How many stories do we have of individuals finding unexpected strength in adversity, undergoing memorable transformative experiences? These are part and parcel of a warrior tradition. When they are part of your culture, part of your existence, they become day-to-day occurrences. The inter-relationship of pain, bravery and respect needs to be examined without our blinkered cultural expectations. In ritual the pain transcends the personal and is shared within the family, with the wider community and with our ancestors. We don't have such rituals, and we have a very confused relationship with pain. Almost all of us are scared of it and take it personally. *'If nothing else, it begins as an awareness of the fear itself. And then, somehow, you pass right through fear, right through the pain. You enter a realm both within and beyond fear and pain. So long as you feel pain, it means you're thinking of yourself. Only when you stop thinking of yourself can you actually get past that pain and that fear. You've got to forget yourself to find yourself. You yourself are the entry way.'*[*6]*   Once you have been through such a process you can come to terms with those things worth being afraid of, and those you can't do anything about. As a culture we spend a lot of our time worrying and being afraid of unimportant things, or things we can do nothing about. That is the behaviour of an uninitiated person.

Gift

A Samburu boy sacrifices himself in the ritual. He is circumcised as a gift to his ancestry, to the elders and the wider community. By being circumcised he is committing himself to stay within his community. He is showing how much respect he has for his ancestors and traditions, and accepting the laws and rules of the tribe. The circumcision is a symbolic acceptance of his responsibilities to the future as well. He is showing how seriously he takes the coming responsibility of parenthood and guardianship of his tribe's land. He is prepared to go through such a depth of pain without flinching, without movement, without anaesthetic. The pain is transcended because of the belief in and acceptance of its significance.

THE PRESENT

It would be impossible to replicate such a barbaric act in our western culture. Indeed it would be wholly inappropriate, because we do not live a nomadic existence and we have no real sense of community or family. It would be very useful to develop our equivalents, and to explore ways of creating and managing them. Unfortunately, at present, the depth of commitment to community is not present in our teenagers. A boy must want to do it. He must come to this conclusion and ask older men to help him to pass through it. If this element isn't present then the rites of passage can be shallow and not of such great value, especially if it is done for him. It must come from within.

On the morning my son, age 16, went to a sweat lodge with older men to welcome him into the start of adulthood, of his own accord, he came in and woke his mother. Kissing her on the cheek he said, 'That's the last time I kiss you as a boy.' You can imagine how much his mother cried. When we sat in the silence and dark of the lodge that afternoon, an unprompted, small, confident voice stated, 'Thank you men for coming here today. You are all the bridge over which I will walk to my manhood.' You can imagine how much we *all* cried that day! But we all acknowledged his wisdom and character.

This acknowledgement defines the rite of passage: it is the recognition of who you are by your elders. Rites of passage are hard, not simple. They do not offer a simple option; indeed, they must be tough. By being so difficult they enable the individual to find the right path. If they were over quickly then the path may not be the right one. If they are too simple, the boy will probably choose the path suggested to him by others – by his parents, peers or school teachers – that is, the path they want him to choose, which suits them, not the one he needs for his own growth and natural development. Parents, peers and schoolteachers can't do this work. These people will impose their views and judgements of the boy before he becomes a man. As I said my mother wanted me to be a doctor, fortunately I was academically so poor I never followed that path, I followed my own. I would have made a very bad doctor, and in the end I still helped lots of people. Instead of leaving this work to parents this rite must be done by elders who have the interests of the individual at heart, but also the interest of the wider community. Their goal is to see the individual recognize who he is, by doing this, he will

100

return to his community and contribute fully. If he doesn't do this properly he will always be doubtful, and that is no good for the community. You can't rely on someone who doubts himself.

The creation of self

The Samburu understand this principle and they have incorporated it into their rites of passage for the braves. After circumcision the young men are trained for fifteen years. They are able to paint and decorate themselves, and they use red ochre to paint and adorn their bodies, particularly their faces. They use beads to decorate and thread their hair. Each warrior may take hours each day decorating and cultivating a particular look for himself. Through doing this he eventually creates a unique image. This includes what he wears, how he stands, where he stands even – it is all about attitude and style. The elders know each brave must do this in order to 'get it out of his system'. Once they have expressed themselves in this way they start wanting to settle down and to have a family, as each generation, or age set, has done for hundreds of years. The Samburu named their present youngest age set L'Kishami, 'the beloved'. The generation before them were the L'Murli, 'the unopposed'. Each generation is named every fifteen years or so, because that is how long it takes the boys to become men, even though they experience the circumcision ritual in the first year. Through this long period of ascent, they create themselves, they express themselves fully and without restriction, and then they come down, into the descent, and are happy to settle down. Again the braves come to this decision by themselves. They aren't forced to it – 'your six months are up, go get a job.' That isn't the way of the Samburu or any indigenous people.

The individual must have fought and battled to find the true path, and in a sense he must have despaired of ever finding it. He must have stepped right into the darkest parts of himself in order to find the true nature of his soul. It's not enough to do this work with only part of your mind or

101

soul. This is wholehearted work, full of despair, failure, achievement, disappointment, desire, pride, ownership and eventual success. When completed there is such a deep sense of success, pride and accomplishment. It is about self-confidence, pride. The individual needs to be proud of himself and to see that his wider community is proud of him, and then he will take pride in that community.

Loyalty and allegiance

During a recent residential event for young people between the ages of 17 and 22, we came across the notion of loyalty. The majority of the participants were from areas of high social need, and their literacy skills were very poor, let alone the academic achievement levels. They arrived on the Friday evening. Only three of them had met before, through that night the noise levels rose as they played, tested and found their equilibrium. Without having slept, we all then worked together in the woods on the Saturday, and the group bonded. In the afternoon of the Saturday we came across another group who were doing similar work in the woods. Suddenly our group, particularly the boys, became very protective. They defended their territory and the group, and didn't want the other group interfering with us. In such a brief amount of time the boys had sorted out their allegiances, pecking order, bonded and formed very strong ties. Despite their academic difficulties, they were very adept at socialising and creating community. For me, this is a typical product of the work I do. Boys create bonds and form groups very quickly, and this is useful in an evolutionary sense. The group collaborates and mutually supports, it defends territories and it very quickly creates identity. The boys identified with us and the work we were doing, despite the fact they had only just met us.

Young men are programmed to do this. We all are. The phenomenon of football fans is a good example. When a young boy identifies with a particular football team and goes to the matches, watches them, meets other supporters, exchanges friendships and has euphoric and disappointing shared experiences, it creates a strong bond. When his team is then relegated and isn't doing so well, he will remain loyal, despite the attraction of supporting the more successful teams. The part-time supporters, who don't attend games and haven't experienced the euphoria and disappointment, are more likely to join with the more successful teams when times are hard. Teams which have a strong fan base can still attract huge numbers of supporters even when they sink to the lower divisions. Loyalty is a very strong impulse, and it creates the communities of the future.

Peer initiation

Our teenagers are trying to make the journey from boy to man without knowing how to do it. Intuitively they are developing rites of passage. They are setting themselves dangerous challenges, stealing cars, taking drugs, taunting women, drinking and fighting. All are expressions of initiation. Individuals are challenged to show how tough they are by undertaking anti-social behaviour. In particular there is a real problem with boys, but it is increasingly a problem with girls as well. At present we are ignoring them, not involving ourselves very well in their lives, so they are initiating themselves into adulthood. This is called peer initiation, and the consequences of this are disastrous. They are devising any number of tests for each other, including:

* *How much alcohol you can consume – every year many young men die from alcohol poisoning due to binge drinking.*
* *What drugs you can take – leading to addictions, criminal activities to support habits, vandalism and antisocial behaviour due to drug induced 'dares'.*
* *Having fights – picking fights with total strangers in the streets or clubs. Again this can often lead to hospitalization and on occasion death.*
* *Driving cars whilst under the influence of drugs or alcohol – again leading to damage of property, hospitalisation and deaths.*

*   *The rape and gang-banging of girls – leading to physical abuse, damage and long-lasting psychological trauma, and again creating huge social problems, depression and suicide.*

*   *Tattooing and body piercing as a means of the creating identity – sometimes this is done with dirty needles and without proper equipment, leading to hospitalization, permanent scarring and poisoning. (Although, who am I to be judgmental? I have many tattoos!)*

*   *Depression, self-mutilation and even suicide can often be the result of 'testing' by self and peers.*

These are just some of the ways in which our young boys are presently becoming men. As a society we have chosen to allow them these options, rather than the safety of a rite of passage under the supervision of older men. We too haven't been initiated, so we don't know how to do this properly; we have forgotten how to do this work well. The costs to the NHS and other services of these peer initiations is measured in millions of pounds per year. We choose to pay this price rather than involve ourselves wholeheartedly in sensible alternatives. We could take the example of the Samburu, which is to give our teenagers access to and time with older men, who could offer guidance and lessons, which could still contain dangerous elements. In reality we have left our teenagers no alternatives, and the rites they have devised are sometimes 'successful'.

Often gangs create a sense of self, pride and a holding place for homeless and hopeless individuals. They generate a sense of belonging which our society has singularly not been able to do. *'Despite the fact that these rituals have had to be invented on the streets, out of necessity, despite the fact that these are peer driven rituals with no 'elders' present, despite the fact that there are no broader community values that provide the structural container within which these state transitions are effected, these rituals are effective. In this post-modern, fragmented age in contemporary America, where the sacred* has been scattered and diffused, there appears to be no center that holds the set of initiation rituals that tries to sustain it.' *7

Too often, and more frequently than not, the products of these peer initiations are toughened and hard men, who feel that emotional intelligence or vulnerability are bad. These are half-baked men. Because they are now accepted as men, they choose to perpetuate the initiation of boys on the next generations. Each generation is stepping further away from emotional intelligence, rather than towards it. This leaves us with a lot of very discontented, angry and confused young boys.

Lack and crisis

Professionals working in the social, health and youth fields are now becoming aware of an acute gap within their provision that needs to be addressed.

How do we work with boys?
How do we include men?
How can we encourage young men to be good fathers?
The answer to these questions lie with the creation of sensible rites of passage for our teenagers, ones which involve the whole community, ones which develop a sense of self, respect and mutual assistance. We have hundreds of thousands of young men who don't know what to do with their lives. The vast majority of them haven't a clue about their soul's purpose. They work in jobs that demean or bore them, often are in addiction and usually lack positive male role models. Many come from families without men, or the men in their lives are involved in crime and immature behaviour themselves. Lacking role models, these boys are now initiating themselves into manhood; they are creating their own peer-led rites of passage.

This basic deficiency in our society is like the oil tanker at sea – turning it around will take a great deal of time, effort and a wide circle. To

105

suddenly create fully integrated rites of passage for teenagers from our inadequate society is asking too much, but we can start to create staging posts and move towards that long-term goal. If we don't, the situation will only worsen. A lot of my time is spent trying to heal the rifts between parents and teenagers, and almost invariably I have to start with the parents. If I can change the behaviour of the parents, then it will affect their relationship to the teenager, and miraculously the teenager will become 'good' not 'bad'.

Here are some examples of the things I have shared:

Good and bad If you say someone is 'bad' enough times, they become it. If you change that and say someone is 'good' and seek to praise their good qualities, they will change (because you have changed!)

Empathize Take time to realize that the three tasks for teenagers are challenging and difficult. Listen to their concerns, wishes and hopes. Spend quality time with teenagers – not your own, but other ones. It will amaze you how complicated, intelligent and brave they are. Bring that back home with you.

It's never too late.... . . to say you are sorry, to build bridges, to listen and learn, to say you love them, to give them a hug, to spend time with them. You are the grownup, so you need to initiate change if you want it.

Talk to them, not at them Tell them about your passions, share your enthusiasms. Tell them how you have been thwarted in the past, explain your disappointments. Don't patronize them – tell it is at it was. Ask them about their dreams, wishes and aspirations, and don't dismiss anything.

Express your appreciation Tell them about how you feel when they do things in a collaborative or loving manner. Be appreciative when they deserve it, and don't do this half-heartedly.

Don't take it personally Remember it's just a phase they're going through. They will not be like this all the time. We all go through such times. Remember what you were like, or how bad some of your friends and acquaintances were. Take deep breaths.

They need role models As a parent you are a role model to your children. However, when they become teenagers they will need different and diverse role models. They are trying to separate from you, so they are naturally looking beyond you and into the wider world. Boys will seek male role models, so provide them with some. If you don't, they will find their own.

They need to make mistakes If we are always protected and cosseted, it is not so easy to learn. It is a lot quicker to learn from our mistakes than our successes, so let them fail. This is a tough lesson for the parents, let alone the teenagers.

Character Teenagers who make mistakes will become interesting grownups. Do you want to restrict and stop your child from developing wholly and completely? In order to do so he needs to experience the shadow as well as the light.

They are always asking the question 'Why?' That's what teenagers do. It is a difficult question to answer, but you can no longer give glib responses. You need to answer them fully, as an adult, not a child. Maybe some of their ideas are actually better than yours! Go on . . . admit it!

They are still very young Please remember this when you see a bunch of kids hanging out on a street corner. They are vulnerable young people despite what they look like. If you have this attitude you are far less likely to be threatened or abused.

Don't try to act, look or talk like them All too often the youth and community workers I share my practice with suffer under the delusion that they can imitate and 'get with' the young people. It is not attractive, and will almost invariably alienate the teenagers you are seeking to connect to.

Be yourself, be honest I remain myself whilst working with teenagers. Indeed I often stress the differences in age and outlook.

Teenagers like me because I know who I am, and I have an opinion. I share my mistakes as well as my triumphs.

Respect is to be won; it is not a given   Many people tell me young people have no respect for their elders. Young people say to me, 'You have to earn respect. Just because you're old doesn't mean you deserve respect.' They respect me when they get to know me, when I have proved my worth. That's how it should be.

Love needs to be given   So many parents focus on the negative. They become depressed and angered by their teenagers 'failure to be successful'. Every cloud has a silver lining. A teenager who takes drugs and has an abortion is still a success – if you believe in them, if you love them.

Touch them   Many parents stop cuddling and comforting their children when they become teenagers. The withdrawal of physical contact between the parents and their teenagers can cause a lot of damage on a number of levels. Many teenagers object to a hug, but please notice how and when they object, i.e. probably in front of others. When you are alone, please continue to offer physical comfort.

The human race is a long one. Please don't prejudge a teenager's success or failure. They still have a long way to go to become a complete human being. The role of the teenager in society is vital. They challenge the establishment. They bring about change, disruption and renewal. Such energetic disruptions are to be encouraged, not stifled, especially given the mess we have created on the planet and within our society. We need to be listening to the next generations.

THE FUTURE

Teenagers are the barometer of health for a culture; they are the product of all our educational, parental and society aspirations. We have spent a lot of time and money influencing our children. We have given them an education, and in this moment – teenagehood – they stand reflecting the wishes of our society as a whole, before becoming part of it. What a sorry state we are in. It seems we want to produce dysfunctional, moody and unhappy people. We suppress and bully our children, when we should be encouraging them to become entrepreneurs and visionaries. Our education system should be geared to enabling our children to find out who they are, and to encourage them to 'live in the flow' as much as possible. To live in the flow is to be yourself, to find what they are uniquely good at. If our teenagers were living in the flow, they could become adults with less problems.

The flow
When we live in the flow-
We are healthier
We are happier
We are more likely to help others
When we are living away from the flow-
We are not content, always seeking
We are more likely to be stressed and unhappy
We are prone to illness, eating disorders, etc.
We are likely to be more selfish and unsociable
When we are working or living in the flow we are adding value to ourselves, our families and the wider community. If we are going to address the crisis in the NHS, the lack of respect in our society and the dysfunctional and addictive behaviour of our population, we need to ensure that more and more people live and work in their flow. The best way to find your flow is to be tested, to undergo a rite of passage. In previous cultures teenagers were tested and, once through that test, they were able to start living in the flow. These rites of passage were recognized as being of paramount importance. They were created in a complex, sophisticated manner. They ensured the individual left home, found friends and sought his life's purpose. Our cultural testing of

ourselves is now so underdeveloped and inadequate that it doesn't encourage our children to leave home, but engenders fear and loathing in them and encourages them to take menial and lowly paid jobs. We need to see the long-term benefits of rites of passage for teenagers. The transition from child to adult is the period in which the flow is identified; this needs to be supported, thought about and maintained for many years. Rites facilitate the creation of a new person, an adult who knows what he or she wants from life. This may be very different from the life of the parents.

SUGGESTIONS FOR ACTION

There are core conditions that need to be present in order for our teenagers to find themselves through a rite of passage:

There must be mentors who know what is possible, who have been through the process themselves, who guide the initiate.

When a young woman gives birth, she is assisted through this important phase by a midwife. The midwife has two principle jobs: to assist with the birth and to teach the new mother how to look after the baby. The midwife is an older woman, not the mother. We need to apply the principles of midwifery to our teenagers. In a sense they are giving birth to themselves as adults, and they need to be assisted and taught at this most important time. When this transition is taught and assisted by older men, it will be a lot easier both on the boy and society as a whole. The benefits from this work are intergenerational and the knock-on effects will be beneficial to the children of the future.

The initiate needs to want to do this work; he must be mature enough to understand that this work is needed.

There is no reason to force people through rites of passage when they are not ready. The whole point of this transition is the willingness of the initiate to participate and for him to see it as necessary. Teenagers join gangs because they want to belong; they find the idea of belonging attractive. Supervised rites of passage for teenagers have to be that attractive!

The initiate must be challenged, must be pushed beyond his normal experience and boundaries. This is how we make the rite attractive to teenagers. The challenges need to be appropriate to the society in which they are being undertaken. The un-anesthetized circumcision of the Samburu boy made sense within their community and the harsh realities of their society. Whilst I was there, 6 people were killed during a raid by a neighbouring tribe to steal cattle. This kind of ritual would be inappropriate here, but we need to develop challenges which are worth taking. The peer initiations that many young men undergo in our inner cities are not holistic. They develop only one aspect of the masculine – the hard and negative side. If we are to make any progress as a species, we need to introduce rites of passage that include more aspects of masculinity, namely, the emotional and vulnerable as well as the physically strong.

He must learn that he needs the help of others, he must learn about reciprocity.
In the coal industry the young man was apprenticed to the old master. There was a reason for this: the old man knew his way around the pit and taught the young man how to navigate the extremely dangerous environment without getting killed. This sums up teenage rites of passage – challenging, supported and worthwhile.

He needs to be away from his family to find his skills and abilities.
He is seeking his soul's purpose, and the only way he will find it is by making mistakes, trying things that don't work, being disappointed, and

111

being hurt. As a parent, can you watch and not interfere as your son does this? It is very difficult. That is why parents can't do this job.

When he has completed this work, he must be acknowledged, praised and welcomed as a new person, not the person who started the rite.
The end of the rite is vital. If he has been through all these trials and tribulations and doesn't receive the acknowledgment he deserves, he will remain a teenager. A great many men have been through their rites and when they return to their parental home their parents keep them in the child place. This can go on for years. Such men are uninitiated. We need to receive the acknowledgment of our parents, our family and our friends to complete the process. Without fail the indigenous peoples around the world make a huge festival in celebration of the completion of the task. Within this feast there was the acceptance of change. On graduation the Samburu boys' families must slaughter two cattle as part of the feast. This is a huge commitment from such cattle-dependent people. By doing this, the parents are showing that they recognize that their son has made the journey from boy to man.

Rites beyond health and safety
This work is beyond the confines of Health and Safety. That is what makes such work worthwhile and precious. However, it also makes it very difficult to gain funding or receive backing from local authorities and charitable trusts. In one ceremony I organized the men involved decided that they needed to wrestle. Normally we have a contract at the beginning of work, and this states 'no violence'. We created a circle, held it with some rhythmical drumming and agreed that anyone who stepped into the space was no longer bound by the contract. It represented a huge challenge to those men who had led pretty safe and protected lives, many of whom had never been involved in a fight before. One by one we stepped inside. After several hours, two broken ribs and many bruises,

112

we finished. This happened years before the book and film *'Fight Club'*, but like this it showed how relevant and important danger and physical challenge is in working with men. Without an element of challenge, fear and the potential of failure, a rite of passage really isn't true. A lot of our teenagers are doing this work already, and a lot of them are hurt and killed because they are unsupervised. It is time we did something about this, and replaced it with supervised challenges and rites. These will take a lot of preparation and training to create and maintain. They are something for the future, but we should be working towards these goals. We must be offering our young people a more viable alternative. There are many ways in which this work can develop and flourish. The seeds of such work are presently being sown – so nurture them.

Example I

During a weekend vision quest ceremony, we took young teenage boys out of their city environments and put them into nature. It would take too long to describe everything here, but they experienced some difficult challenges – being woken at 5:30am in November, being sent out into the dark wilderness as the snow fell! They survived, and we went on to work intensely with them around the concepts of mystery, the unknown and the magical. As teenagers they struggled with these concepts. Their astutely developed left-sided, logical brains fought us every step of the way. We weren't making much progress, when one evening I said, 'Tonight you are going to dream. When you wake up, I want you to write the dream down immediately.' They dreamed and wrote them down. We asked them to describe their dreams. One had dreamed he was in a fairground, and was asked by people he was familiar with, but didn't know, to try out the attractions. As he went from ride to ride he continued to meet friendly people he recognized and yet didn't know. Finally, he had tried and mastered every ride he was given a t-shirt from his favourite band as reward. I was so pleased, I asked, 'So what does this dream mean?' He spent a little time thinking, then replied, 'I like fairgrounds?' I almost pulled my hair out at that moment. We worked with another dream, and suddenly we could see the boy was starting to understand the symbolic nature of his nocturnal experiences. We went back over the dream, and he was able to explain it beautifully, and very poetically. He felt it reflected his experience with us. Finally, he said, 'And now I know why I know those people, because they were aspects of myself, they were parts of me.' He had cracked it.

Example 2

At the end of a ceremony, the participants were blessed by a young teenage boy and girl. This was very moving and a real privilege, as all too often teenagers are excluded from such rituals. The boy spoke of his thanks to the elders of his tribe for being prepared to do ceremony for him. He was a particularly vulnerable and yet toughened boy, with a very troubled background. As the ceremony broke up I realized the men involved needed to honour him, so we took him off to a dark place. I wanted to honour the way in which he had been able to talk in front of such a large crowd.

From somewhere in my heart came an urge, and I tend to go with such things. I jumped on him, held him down on the ground. He fought me, I pressed down on him, and a very angry, scared look came across his face. The other men followed my lead, and we pinned him to the floor in dark silence. My face was pressed tight against his, looking hard into his eyes. I said quietly and with authority, 'I see you, I know you, I know what you did.' He squirmed with fear and apprehension, used to being admonished. 'I saw you being brave, I love you for being such a brave young man, I love you for being such a good talker in front of so many people...' On I went. His face relaxed, his breathing eased off, he smiled and started to laugh. The rhythm of his laughing body was connected to all of ours, and we all melted into a laughing heap in the dark.

We showed him a 'grief bundle' we had wrapped in cloth, and explained how we had grieved the bundle into existence. For us the bundle represented abuse, shame and the corruption of power, and our wish to stop such things. We didn't want to pass them on to the next generation. We had undertaken the work so that he didn't have to carry the burden on. It was a very emotional moment for us all. He helped us bind the bundle up. We said we trusted him. We gave the bundle to him, and asked that he bury it for us. No one went with him – it was a commission of trust. He was very proud about being given such an important task. These stages of the ceremony were completely unplanned, yet they complemented all that had gone before. It was very moving and beautiful. If we hadn't seized the opportunity he would not have been honoured.

Example 3

In 2009, we took three groups out into the wilderness and worked on creating new names for each of the individuals. This was three-phase venture. First, the individuals had to come to terms with any negative names they had received from friends, teachers, relatives and family, to accept what had happened. They then went out on their own into the wilderness and spent time alone. There they were able to go through the names, and appreciate the 'golden lining' in them. They returned with a new, positive and affirming name, their 'future potential' name. As elders we welcomed them back and confirmed their names. This was a very moving and transformative process for the young men, and I'll just tell one story of the many incidents along the way.

One event was held on a remote farm in the very beautiful Derbyshire countryside. I'd never used the site before, so I was unsure what to expect. The farmer informed me we would be fine – the group could camp with the cows. I was a little perturbed by this news, as I have experienced cows trampling tents and causing problems, but I thought I'd go with the flow. A day before the event I phoned the farm to confirm everything, and was casually told, 'The cows and the bull are in the field.' The bull! As it was too late to change, we camped with the bull. I had never before been in such close proximity to such an impressive beast. What a privilege it was. How the boys learnt from the experience. It was beautiful – a weekend about being male, sharing it with an immense teacher, who let us know very firmly who was in charge and on what terms we were temporarily in his field.

A prayer for the future

How we create the next steps and rites will be vital for our survival on this planet, I am absolutely convinced of that. So, I look forward with anticipation and great expectation to the next twenty years of creativity, collaboration and humble adventures. May all men know they have a role and responsibility to the planet, and may they work in peace and harmony to co-create a future full of compassion, empathy and love in collaboration with the women of this world. May we also learn how to celebrate, how to give thanks correctly. Unreserved, unconditional expressions of community celebration are rare but extremely beautiful things. May we all be able to find our way back to such expressions, and may we share them with our children.

Community

So many people bemoan the loss of community as being one of the major reasons for our present problems. As a community artist I was employed all over the world to create artefacts of beauty with large groups of people. These murals told the people's stories, and gave them an opportunity to express themselves. A hugely important part of the process was the celebration on completion. Everyone involved – their families, their friends – came together and gave praise. Such events create community. It can be a community lasting for one day, or a lifetime. All I can say is that those individuals will remember them for a long time. Part of building community is the mutual support inherent in celebration. I know it is vital, and that creativity and celebration are the glue binding a community together. We need to remember and recreate this. Rites of passage are ideal starting points.

10

Rite of passage
Couvade

The Lesson
Responsibility

The Age
Father

South West

The colour of **Purple**
Royal and responsible

118

THE FIFTH AGE
Father

For whatever reason, adolescence appears to be the young man's default state, proving what anthropologists have discovered in cultures everywhere: it is marriage and children that turns boys into men.
Kay S. Hymowitz

I am the father of two beautiful children. They will always remain my children despite the fact they are both now in their twenties. Until I became a father I let life happen to me, I was a surfer on the crest of waves, I rode and glided. Once I became a father I behaved differently: I made things happen, I created opportunities, I rose to challenges. My children gave me a huge amount of blessings, love, hope and joy. In many ways my life was a practice and a rehearsal until the day my first child was born, then it became real.

THE RITE OF PASSAGE
Couvade
Separation - *From the single life, he explores sexuality, and in its exploration he discovers femininity (internal and external)*
Transition - *He seeks someone to complete him*
Incorporation - *He becomes the father of a child, he takes the responsibility*

The first four ages, from foetus to teenager, are temporary; they are phases we pass through. When we become a man there is a certainty to it. We should not choose to revert to the previous ages, although many men do. During the course of these early years we will have experienced a great deal of abundance, pleasure, awe and excitement. Equally, we will have been disappointed, angry, abandoned, sad and fearful, and we will have lost things. We will have been positive and negative. The awareness and experience of these two creates the whole person, creates a man worth knowing. Thus far the growth has been one way – we have become a man by fully exploring masculinity. The next age is approached through our femininity, the internal and external female. This brings about a change. From being self-centred, we seek a partner, someone to 'complete' us. The rite of passage into fatherhood is very subtle and complex, and needs a good deal of explanation. I will explain what needs to happen from two perspectives – when we are wounded and the ceremony of couvade.

Wounding

In the ideal, the teenager is taken away from his mother and he lives with men. He does this in order to find himself during his 'bravery' rite. As discussed in the last chapter, the challenge can make him hard. This next rite reverses that process. *'After the resistance to identification with the Mother that characterizes a young man's initiation rites comes the ironic reversal of preparation for fatherhood: he must locate mother in his own body.'*[*8] The archetype which is used in a great many stories is that of the warrior, king or hero – call him whom you will. He is happy living a life of ascension, moving upwards and out into the world. His journey is one of power and thrusting masculinity. When he is maturing, not when he is a teenager, he receives a wound; he is cut. This cut is almost invariably to the thigh, and represents the womb. Zeus carries the baby Dionysos in the wound on his thigh. The wounding of the hero is associated with descent, the slowing down of life and the internalization of the event or

120

experience, which can lead to the individual becoming despondent or broody. *'The King's men galloped after him, and one got close enough to give him a leg wound with the end of his sword. The young man escaped; but his horse made such a powerful leap to do so that the young man's helmet fell off, and everyone could see he had golden hair.'*[9] The young man is wounded in his thigh, and his identity is revealed. This means he can no longer pretend; he has to become his true self. A very necessary part of the process is introspection. Paradoxically the wounded man becomes more whole and complete. He now needs to undergo the next rite of passage.

Couvade

Couvade is not a very helpful word, coming as it does from the French word for 'cowardly incapacity', so I need to explain it more fully. It was first used in anthropological studies of indigenous people during the early 1800s. These early (all male) anthropologists encountered different types and forms of couvade on every continent of the planet. Very few anthropologists actually met indigenous people, most sat in museums. Through the course of such flawed research they uncovered various baffling (to them) rituals. These offended their sense of masculinity and so they labelled them 'cowardly incapacity'. Examples came from the Aboriginal people of Australia, the native peoples of India and the Americas and, particularly, inhabitants of the Celtic and Basque countries of Europe. The rite was seen as the feminizing of the man, something these Victorian gentlemen couldn't understand, didn't see the value of, and were vehemently opposed to. In light of this personal aversion, unsurprisingly, very few rituals were documented correctly or explained in depth. Reading between the lines, the overriding principles were as follows:

The prospective father would be mentored prior to birth. An elder would tutor him in the ways of couvade appropriate to his culture. This mentor was the male equivalent of the midwife.

The prospective father would incapacitate himself by lying down during the last days of his partner's pregnancy.

He would forsake violence, put down all weapons and wear loose clothing with no knots.

During the birth he would either be encouraged or forced (depending which culture he was from) into the sharing of his partner's pain.

Immediately after birth he would accept the baby and lie with it in his bed. In many traditions he was fed and showered with gifts.

These diverse rituals were so ridiculous to Victorian sensibilities that they have been all but removed from our cultural heritage and history, and the practice of couvade is now extinct, as far as I can tell. The rite was at its strongest and lasted the longest in Europe. To quote the Victorians is to hear the echoes of their disdain for such a custom:

Lapland

'To put a handle on an axe in the house of a lying-in woman was impious. The Laplanders cautiously provided against anything twisted or knotted in the garments of a person under such a situation, led by a vain imagination that such knots would render the birth of the woman more difficult.'

America

'When childbirth overtakes the wife, the husband puts himself to bed, and there, grunting and groaning, affects to suffer all the agonies of a woman in labour. Lying there, he is nursed and tended for some days as carefully as though he were the actual sufferer.'

The Luzonz tribes of Bontok area in the Philippine islands

'When a woman has given birth to a child, she must go with it to the river, wash it and herself, and return to the settlement, hand the child over to the father, and go on with her work. She only has it back to give it the breast; the man nurses it, carries it wrapped in a covering on his back, and receives the visits of friends and acquaintances whilst the woman works in the fields.' *10

Such dismissive writing has meant we are left without an inkling of how tender, beautiful and sharing such rites must have been. Nor Hall, in his astonishing book *Broodmales*, attempts to give us a little insight into the depth and beauty of couvade. In his description of a Mexican Huichol yarn painting called *How the Husband Assists in the Birth of the Child*, Hall writes that the man *lies as the woman does, outstretched. He radiates golden energy on a purple field perhaps cut off from her physically (lying inside the hut while she lies outside on the ground). They are intimately and essentially connected by the life cord tied around his genitals and extending downward toward her open palms, thus displaying an exquisite sensitivity to each other in the birth moment. Below their navels, the tripartite form of the brown child mirrors the dark fruit of the father's sex. As the attendants reach for the emerging child, the chain of life lengthens: the blood blanket around its small form is the same vibrant red as their heart swaths. All of nature is connected in the male and female reach of the event. Even the plants extend towards each other – tendrils toward fruit – resembling the open, root-exposed pose of the birthing parents.*[11]

Now that's what I call couvade!

Modern couvade syndrome

At the same time as discovering these gems I came across further references to couvade, but using the word in a different context. Scientists are piecing together a very interesting picture in terms of how the prospective father is affected mentally, physically and psychologically by his partner's pregnancy, and they are calling this 'couvade syndrome'. The research is worldwide and the conclusions are beginning to take shape as follows:

* *Up to 60% of men are affected either psychologically or physically by their partner's pregnancy.*
* *In the man, there can be a rise in oestrogen and a decline in testosterone, particularly during the third trimester.*
* *Some have morning sickness, nose bleeds, bloating and enlarged nipples.*
* *Some know their partner is pregnant before they do.*

The majority of men talk of their partner's pregnancy and the sharing of birth and early childhood as being a 'wake-up call'. They change their lifestyle, friends, job and attitudes towards life.

Oestrogen
The link between testosterone increasing when we step through the bravery rite of passage, and the increase in oestrogen during the couvade rite is very informative. All of this scientific research just backs up what our ancestors knew all those years ago. The man is contacting his internal female. He is increasing his oestrogen in order to be able to support and help his partner. The descriptions of couvade and the concept of wounding inspire and excite me. If we as a society can start to create new ways of encouraging the future father to slow down and contemplate, and by doing so support his partner through birth, we would really be changing our present culture.

How many of our present woes in terms of wild young boys and men comes back to their lack of fathering, the absent fathers who have not bonded with their babies or their children?

When did we last put the father to bed and place the naked baby on his chest so the first sweat he tastes is male (Greek tradition)?

When did we last say to the potential father, 'share your partner's pain'?

When did we shower the father with gifts and blessings?

Reclaiming couvade
Working with midwives we run retreats for expectant couples, during which we enable the men to explore the concept of couvade and develop their own relationship to it, helping them understand how they can be active and engaged in a masculine way with the pregnancy, birth and early childhood cycle. We've started reclaiming couvade, and maybe in time we'll come up with a far better name for it. It represents a great opportunity to create and develop a rite for men in terms of their passage into fatherhood – now there's a challenge worth taking! As with

all these rites and ages they can be archetypal as well as practical and physical. So if a man has decided he will not become a father, he can still go through the rite of couvade, contacting his inner female. It does not exclude him from learning the lesson of 'being a father'. The passage through couvade teaches all of us a very simple lesson, namely, that by passing through the rite you come to responsibility. You have to take responsibility not just for yourself but for a helpless and dependent baby. This changes your life forever.

THE LESSON
Responsibility

The teenage rite enables the boy to become the man. During this transition he is able to explore who he is and what he is good at. The rite of passage he will undertake has a high-risk challenge to it – he will have been severely tested. The combination of overcoming such a challenge and getting to know himself means he has known the ups and the downs of life. In the archetype of this we talk about him having ascended away from his mother at great speed and being wounded; now slowing down, he experiences descent. As we have seen, the next rite, couvade, is about coming to terms with his femininity, his vulnerability, the emotional self, as well as his masculinity. This combination creates the third, a baby. The creation of the third has wide ranging consequences and impacts deeply on his life.

He starts to settle down and create stability in his life. He accepts and, indeed, seeks responsibility. These are the actions of an initiated man, someone who has successfully integrated the previous ages into his life. Unfortunately, because we chose to lose our connection to these simple principles, a great many men have not reached this far in their development when they become fathers. They tumble into fatherhood uninitiated, without male role models, and as a consequence they feel alone, bewildered and lost. They are immature, often unable to cope with the responsibility of fatherhood in its multiplicity of forms. This reflects the incomplete and uninitiated society we have created. The consequences are all around us, and we bemoan them on a regular basis.

I have a friend who was a regular drinker of immense amounts of alcohol, and his capacity was legendary. He was transformed by the arrival of his first-born child. Through the closeness of his relationship with his wife and daughter he started to stay at home and not go out. His drunken mates became so upset about this change that they rowdily woke him late at night to shout insults at him from his front garden. By doing so they woke and frightened the baby and wife and infuriated him – not advisable. Their reaction was typical of the uninitiated man.

Yin and Yang

In order to enter into a relationship with the female our father-to-be needs to comprehend the significance of his actions, and the Yin and Yang symbol has been used for thousands of years as a means of understanding exactly this. He can only become a father by entering a relationship with a woman, and he needs to understand what that means.

YIN and YANG - *Taoism's Dance of Opposites*

126

This is not a religious symbol – it is not attached to any religion or group – and I am just using it as a metaphor. It is a symbolic representation of harmony, and tells us about love.

On one level it represents the existence of two things, black and white. When those two things are brought together, their fusion inevitably creates a third. That third is the combination of the two, which didn't exist before. When black and white come together in this way they create black and white, not grey.

It is a very particular shape – a circle, not a square. Why not just have two equal sides to a square? For me the circle represents nature, the natural way of being. We are being shown how to join things in a natural way.

The S–shaped join is particular as well. It represents the way in which fluids mix. It represents motion or change. There is a fluidity to the symbol.

The image can be seen as the globe, and the rotation of the globe past the sun, one side in daylight, the other at night.

It is the mix of two opposites, day and night. When two opposites come together they can fight, they can stagnate or they can mix and combine. This symbol represents hope and love, not conflict and opposition to change.

The symbol is a metaphor for the joining of two. The fusion of the two creates the third, and the whole symbol comes to represent 'motion'. It is a two-dimensional representation of a three-dimensional concept. Without the addition of motion or change, the two will stagnate; they will not flow and mix correctly.

If we look at the symbol as a metaphor for a relationship – the union of the man and a woman – it becomes the joining of two opposites in a mutually respectful manner. Equality is present. The Taoist name for it means the 'dance of opposites'.

The symbol represents the moment of conception, the joining of the egg and the sperm. It is the moment of change.

Within each side there is a dot of the opposite. This represents the ability of the sperm to create a girl, and the ability of the egg to create a boy – the past of the man and the woman, the potential that is carried through into the moment of conception from pre-conceptual circumstances.

127

The symbol represents the way in which a natural and loving relationship between a man and woman, or two people, can be viewed. It is a flowing, mutually supportive interaction, with no sharp lines, no harsh divides; the flowing motion of exchange and interrelation, with growth and change as an integral part.

Within my work I use the symbol to show light and shadow in terms of male and female behavioural patterns. If we represent the negative aspects of maleness as the large black shape, what qualities are present? *Aggression, violence, anger, etc.* In this case what is the small white dot? *Self-confidence, motivation, drive, ambition, etc.* The potential for good in bad. If we represent the positive aspect of femaleness as the large white shape, what qualities are present? *Caring, sharing, nurturing, etc.* In this case what is the small black dot? *Smothering, over-protection, resistance to change, etc.* The potential for bad in good.

The opposites dance together, male and female come together, and by doing so, two become three: the child is born.

The learning curve

As with the teenager, we expect our men to adapt and become fathers without instruction, support and guidance. The age of fatherhood is a long one, with a diversity of influences and a plethora of experiences and developments. Fathering a baby is very different to fathering a child. Our ancestors knew that couvade ensured that the father bonded with the baby. This is the first and probably most important part of taking responsibility. The father is introduced to his baby and he feels at ease with him. I show young fathers how to bond with their baby, and I admit to them that when my first child was born I felt out of my depth. I felt exposed, unable to cope and as though no-one could help me. That is a very common place for first-time fathers. The obvious antidote to such a feeling is to reintroduce the concept of couvade. Literally giving the baby

128

to him and saying, 'there you are, get on with it'. Many young fathers tell me:
* *They are side-lined and feel inadequate during the birth and particularly in the first days after birth.*
* *The focus of attention is on the mother and baby; they feel bewildered.*
* *They find it difficult to bond with the baby, and often find it difficult to bond again with their partner.*

One of the most commonly expressed difficulties for fathers is the idea that they are now restricted, unable to behave in the ways they used to. They feel this has a negative impact on their lives. This shows two things for me: (1) they probably haven't really explored themselves fully and don't know what they want from life (they are not in the flow) and (2) they are unsure about their relationship to the mother. When the father is given responsibility he can feel lonely, unsure and without guidance; he can easily slip into feeling angry and then he wants someone to blame. He knows he should be feeling up to the task and full of hope, but he doesn't; so he blames himself, his partner, his baby for these changes. Here we find the shadow aspects of responsibility. The immature or uninitiated man shirks his responsibility and continues to go surfing, drinking down the pub or playing with his mates. The mature man accepts that he needs to now behave differently.

Response and ability

I feel the true nature of the word *responsibility* can be found in its component parts: *response* and *ability*. The mark of a man is his ability to respond to change, to be able to go with the flow and continue developing. The majority of our uninitiated young men don't want to 'grow up', and this reflects our youth-obsessed and individualized culture. The obvious and delightful aspects of being responsible are very important to the future of our culture. The benefits of being a father are well worth listing:

129

*   *He is in a loving and caring relationship with his partner, and there is a mutual trust, knowledge and respect within the relationship.*
*   *He knows who he is, doing a job he is good at, has found what his soul longs to do, and is pursuing such a vocation.*
*   *This means he is not an apprentice anymore but a skilled worker, someone who can be relied or depended upon.*
*   *He takes on these jobs and sees them through, takes responsibility for their completion and is reliable.*
*   *He knows what he can do and what he can't do. He takes risks, but he also calculates likelihoods, and he judges well.*
*   *He is secure, is always there and can be relied upon to give of his best.*
*   *When he does something, there is an authority to his actions. He is able to explain why and how he does things.*
*   *He is responsible for his partner and his children, and he takes on the ability to respond to their needs and the needs of his wider family.*

These are admirable and very worthy characteristics to have in any human being. They ensure continuity and safety within our society and they are the bedrock on which communities are formed. Our men folk need to aspire to such principles, not shy away from them. The essence of the father is to accumulate. He draws to him those things that are necessary to ensure safety. The accumulation of knowledge, goods, housing, etc. is all part of the role of father. He needs to do this for a long period of time – many years – in order to ensure his children can then move out of the home. He does this in the knowledge that it is just a phase he has to go through. He won't accumulate all his life, he doesn't have to bear the same responsibilities all his life and he will eventually step beyond this phase and into a different lifestyle. I had a friend who lived in 'tipi valley' in Wales and who had only ever lived in temporary tents, yurts or benders. He became a father, and within three months he'd moved into a flat. When I remarked on this very obvious change, he was shocked. He'd not been conscious of it. He also gained regular employment and accumulated furniture and artefacts. His children are now in their early teens and he's back in a yurt.

The introduction of a baby into the relationship can have radical and far-reaching implications. The bonding of the father with the baby is essential. As the baby grows, the balance of the father's work and life is important in the development of a healthy relationship with his children. The provision of safety and material goods is useful, but the child needs time and affection more than anything else. In the early years the child will naturally focus on the mother, but around the age of 5 the child can turn and look for assistance and teachings from the father. He needs to be there and ready to do such work. The child then switches his focus from the parents to his peers as he steps into teenagehood, but the father still needs to be there. Throughout fatherhood the communication of emotional and other needs to the mother is the basis on which positive parenting is founded. The two, the mother and father, have become one. They have become parents, and, ideally, they need to act in harmony in order to provide everything their child needs.

The birth of a child can affect the sexual relationship between the father and the mother. Once the baby is born the sexual bond is severely tested. Instead of there just being the two of them, there are three or more of them. Many things change, and these can affect the sexual relationship:
* *The mother (and father) can be tired, worn out, not in the mood*
* *The mother often feels fat, her body distorted; self-image and self-worth can be affected*
* *The baby can take up lots of their time, which previously was theirs alone*
* *Friends, family and relatives can interfere and take over*
* *Stress and anger can be suppressed and left to fester, as there is no time to discuss things*

These factors can lead to damage being done between the mother and father, and can result in them splitting up. When I work with young first-time couples I always advise:

The changes that have occurred are not permanent; it will not always be like this

Take your time

Try to find time when the two of you can be together, alone, without anyone else, even if it is just for half an hour

Relax in those moments; don't spend that time cleaning the house or rowing; pamper each other

All of us are changing in our body shape; love what is, don't push and seek something that is unattainable or really hard work

You were in a special relationship before the baby came, and that relationship still exists, so don't lose sight of it

THE AGE
Father

The father is a full-grown man not a teenager. He has left home, found his soul's purpose and is now responsible for others. On the physical side, there is nothing more to develop; indeed it is downhill from now on in! However, in the spiritual, psychological and intellectual spheres he is now stepping into a rapid period of learning, creating and becoming. He is actualizing his potential, becoming more than just a bloke, and he is contributing to society. Psychologically he is taking responsibility for not only himself but for others as well. He has to adapt to this, and to change his behaviour accordingly. Fathers are essential to humanity. They provide a vital and hugely important part of our society. When they are missing, the consequences are dire. As J. Embling said, *"I often look around for the fathers in the lives of our children. I feel a sense of profound loss, of defeat, of inhumanity, as I see men devoid of personal contact with their children. Their loss, the loss of something central to human process, is also our loss. Something is being crippled, and all the money,* *technology, bureaucracy, professionalism, ideology in the world won't make it right again." *[12]*

Fathering

To father is to care. It is innately connected to the role of mother. The mother nurtures, the father protects. They are very much the same thing, just seen from a slightly different perspective. We are quite happy to expect the mother to nurture intuitively; the same is true for men. Fathers protect in the same intuitive way. With a group of female social and care workers, we examined the behaviour of fathers compared to mothers and we came to the conclusion that it is only breast-feeding which separates the sexes. All other ways of caring can be undertaken by either sex with equal skill. The only distinctions were minor and based on individuals and biases. The group agreed that when a father cares he can tend to take a few more risks, possibly be more spontaneous. They identified the father as being a solid figure, one who 'remains in the same place', which led us to the concept of consistency. Examples of more laid-back fathers were counteracted by examples of tyrants and disciplinarians. Some even admitted that the father bonded first with the child, and had been more confident from the start than they had been. In the end, we came to a consensus about the qualities of a father:

* *He protects – by providing a safe environment, by working, by teaching, and by playing*
* *He is consistent – by being reliable, always there, present in his children's lives*
* *He is supportive – to his partner by backing her judgments, and also to his children*

These are the qualities we are seeking in the present and next generations of fathers. We do not need:

* *The tyrant – who uses violence, inappropriate anger, verbal or physical abuse directed at his partner or children*

*   *The doormat – who has no opinions, who allows his children to get away with everything, who is unprepared to make decisions which are unpopular*
*   *The absent father – who doesn't fight for and believe in his right to have access to and spend time with his children, no matter what the circumstance*

The fathers of our recent past cast a strong shadow over the expectations for the future. The father provides for the next generation and engenders unconditional love. He doesn't have to have a family and child to be in this frame of mind. A great many men substitute work for a child, for example. Many are self-employed and nurture and protect their companies in this fatherly way. It all comes back to responsibility. At a point in a man's life, he seeks to take responsibility, and by doing so he grows and becomes more whole.

THE PAST
Greeks and Romans
To know how fathers used to be is to step into mythology. There seems to be a consensus around strong, powerful, caring men. The Greek and Roman Gods were fathers, and the father has been closely connected to God for thousands of years. Hopefully he is a benevolent spirit, balancing strength and love with being protective. Unfortunately, an element of this, the shadow aspect of it, is the tyrant. The tyrant is a huge, powerfully built giant, who physically intimidates with his size, and also intimidates with his mind. One trait of the tyrant is his belief that he carries a map of where everything is in his head. He is certain he knows where he is at any given time; all he has to do is consult this internal map. For him, this map never lies. So when he and his family come to a crossroads, one route easily shorter and more well-trodden, the other much longer through a thorn-bush-filled field, and his internal map tells him to go through the field, he will go, and he will drag his family with him. They will arrive at the destination battered, torn, in despair and

134

much later than others, and yet he will never concede he was wrong. When confronted with dissent, the tyrant only becomes angrier and angrier. This is an aspect of the father, not a pleasant one, but nevertheless it exists. The father is determined, driven and stubborn. This can be a very good thing, or a very bad thing; it is just a matter of degrees, and the difference between them is very thin. By being determined, he is showing his love; he is providing for his family. Those who step beyond this into tyranny are uninitiated. They haven't been wounded, they haven't been through couvade. The tyrant inhabits a land of ascent, climbing ever upwards, never looking back, never taking stock. If he had been initiated he would have taken stock, become despondent or broody. In this internal time he would have come to terms with his mistakes and admitted them. He wouldn't then drag his family through the thorns, but accept the alternatives and not be diminished. The tyrant wants to remain huge; he fears diminishment. We live in a tyrannical society. We are fixated on being the best, being young, being strong.

Victorians

The Victorians, who still influence our culture so strongly, admired the qualities of the tyrant, and propagated the idea that the father should become one. The use of discipline, physical and verbal abuse, the aloof nature, the insistence on having the final word, the disconnection from joy, became standard issue with fatherhood. This is a terrible legacy and we still bear the scars. From Victorian tyranny through to today's absent fathers, our society has a lot of work to do in terms of understanding and changing for the better.

World Wars and the Baby Boomers

The First and Second World Wars bred a very particular type of man. Stoical and distant, he suppressed the horrors he had seen in an attempt to protect his children from the immensity of war. A very admirable sentiment, but it caused them a lot of emotional and psychological

135

damage, and affected their relationships with their children. The baby boomer generation didn't go to war, and reacted against their perceived emotionally stunted parenting. The '60s generation were angry and resentful about their fathers, and turned to alternative ways of being, some very useful and some maybe not so useful. As with all human behaviour, there is a constant motion and change involved – one generation reacts, the next compensates, and on it goes.

THE PRESENT
Absent fathers

Absent fathers are a huge issue. They are reported in the press and media and seen to be a bad thing. The common perception goes along familiar lines – they're all lazy men, who could make everything all right again if they were to show some commitment, especially financial. I would caution against such populist propaganda: it is never that simple. The reasons a father is absent from his child's life can be complex. For a start, there are many men who do not know that they are fathers – they are absent because the mother has not told them. There are fathers who choose to donate sperm. A percentage of these are gay, and most are not active in the lives of their children. There are biological fathers who deliberately won't involve themselves in their children's lives. A very small percentage of these are of the opinion their input is not needed, and they are not prepared to change their lifestyle just because they have become a father. Many of those men have been influenced by their peers, their family or by the mother in taking such an attitude.

The mother rejecting the father is also a very common phenomenon. She may exclude him because their relationship has broken down, she has found someone else, the father is abusive or violent, she moves away and many other reasons. The way in which the father responds to this can be on a wide scale – from fighting desperately to retain contact to not bothering. The majority try at the start, but over 40% have given up after 2 years. They do this because circumstances change – perhaps the father finds a new relationship and his new partner doesn't want him involved with his first 'marriage', perhaps they separate over a wide geographical distance, perhaps the job and work circumstances change or perhaps the children say they don't want him in their lives. Then we have the plethora of scenarios in terms of stepfathers, boyfriends and relationships. The biological father can also be a stepfather or male role model to a wide range of children. Only a very small percentage of absent fathers are good-for-nothing men who don't care, please remember that! The job description of father now involves any level of commitments, and the 'normal' one of being the father to 2.4 children is fractured and lies broken. Men have to learn anew what it means to be a father in this post-modern society.

The increase in absent fathers obviously affects the diversity of single-parent families out there. The popular perception of single-parent families is that of the benefit-claiming teenage mothers who shouldn't have become pregnant in the first place. Again this represents a very tiny percentage of the actual truth. Please try to see beyond the simplistic headlines in newspapers. Almost a third of all families in the world are headed by single mothers now. The reasons in developing countries are different to ours – divorce is not as common as desertion, death and imprisonment. The present situation is very murky and unclear. However, that should not deter us from attempting to build a better and more complete picture of the future generations to come. A single parent family can be much better than a no-parent family, and many are very caring, loving and beneficial for the children. Surely, having one parent who is happy is better than having two parents who are physically and emotionally violent with each other.

Prisons

We try to encourage fathers in prisons to retain contact with their children. They frequently do not bother, as they are excluded by the very nature of their incarceration, and also by a wide range of other factors. Many of them don't know even where their children live. So we run programmes where the inmates continue to contact their children despite this. They write cards on the child's birthday and at Christmas. Instead of sending them, they collect them. They also write stories, speak on film, make little comedy sketches, a whole range of very personal and moving creative activities. The fathers keep all of this in the hope that one day, maybe when the child reaches 18, they might want to come and visit their absent father. Instead of not being able to say he thought of them, he will have the evidence; he will be able to say, 'this is how much I still loved you, despite our not being in touch'.

Right now a great many men are not stepping up to their responsibility. In our culture we have a great many uninitiated men. They haven't been through rites of passage, they haven't found their soul's purpose, and they are floundering and unstable. These young men are then becoming fathers. The sudden and life transforming changes which occurs in fatherhood come as a cold shock to their systems. Those in menial or unfulfilling jobs seek to gain their thrills elsewhere, and fatherhood comes as a huge restriction to these perceived freedoms. We have a great many broken and fractured families around, because men are not prepared to take the responsibility that comes with fatherhood. That is a tragedy.

The separation of the mother from the father can also be a blessing. When the father is violent or abusive the mother needs to take action to safeguard herself and her children. Frequently, the father is not violent until a baby changes the relationship. Domestic violence is far more prevalent than we think. It doesn't just affect working class families, but is through all classes. The use of violence and abuse in the suppression of women is widespread all over the world. Education and remedial actions are needed. This reflects a fundamental failing in our culture. It shows our lack of maturity – violence always reflects insecurity and a lack of responsibility. We must seek to act positively to change the situation in the future.

THE FUTURE

How to liberate without also destroying, how to make free without also making horror and devastation? This is the big internal and external problem of our culture, and until we have come up with answers we cannot claim to be a post-patriarchal world. Instead of Herakles who cuts, clubs and slays, why can't we emulate the style of, say, Hermes, who outwits, outruns, and slips out of sight? If men are caught up in the invisible knot of the mother-complex, why not deftly slip out of the knot like the trickster Houndini, rather than blast away at the knot like the slasher Rambo? Men today are called upon to look for new, more subtle and progressive styles of psychic liberation. A consciousness of the future must be less confrontational and macho, and more hermetic or trickster-like. [*13]

The remodelling of the father along these lines is essential to the development of a more caring and realistic culture. In order to achieve this, a major transformation is needed and as with all revolutions we have to start small in order to think big. The next generation of fathers need to have a mentor, or mid-husband, comparable to the wife having a midwife. This mentor should coach and guide the father before the birth, and especially after. This job cannot be done by his own father; it has to be seen as being an important and valuable job in its own right, just like a midwife. The mentor puts the father through the relevant couvade ritual. By doing so he ensures the bonds between the father and the baby are as strong as possible. Even given these conditions there will be absent fathers in the future, but at least this will start to address the problem.

However, the job of mentoring the father will be more complex than just showing him how to be with a baby. The potential father needs to know what it is to be responsible. He can only do this if he has found what he is good at. He needs to see how important the next stage of his life will be. He needs to see that it is the end of some the ascent and carefree lifestyle and the beginning of responsibility, joy, sharing and being loved, all of which compensate completely for the perceived loss of freedom.

The blackbird

About 10 years ago, I wrote the following piece on the male blackbird, which at the time was just an observation of nature: *The blackbird is a skulker. He scuttles under trees, in bushes, under cover. He spends the great majority of his time hidden deep in the undergrowth, and there he is silent, secure, safe and protected. In the early morning, and at the end of the day, he steps out of the cover and flies to the top of the nearest tree. Completely out of character, he sits exposed for the whole world to see, and sings. He sings a song of astonishing beauty, passion, power, of humility. His song resonates through the woods and is listened to and admired by all that hear it. In those moments he exposes himself, he becomes the full self, he is the complete bird, he is in his power. The raiding buzzards or goshawks could easily come and pick him off at this time, and yet even they seem nonplussed by this bravery, by this totemic display of who he is. He steps out into the world and claims to be who he really is, not the skulker. How much better for all of us, if every man, twice a day, stepped up, and proclaimed himself, stood in his humble power, and enhanced the world with the beauty of his song or being.* This is the father, the humble servant of a biological imperative. His natural urges and the compunctions of his DNA take him to a new, dangerous and yet liberating place. This is how we need our fathers to be right now and in the future.

Benefits of active fathers

Together with Tony Ivens, I have written a book called *An Introduction to Working With Fathers*, which documents many of the benefits of having active fathers for children. I want to re-state some of our conclusions:

* *If we could reintroduce the ritual of couvade then the father would connect to his inner female through their understanding and respect for his partner.*

* *After the ritual, we need to honour and congratulate him, to ensure that he stays with the child for the long haul.*

* *He needs to lie in bed with his newborn and to have it taste his sweat. This may seem extreme, but I think the bonding consequences of such an action were well observed by our ancestors.*

* *If the father were to accept that becoming a father will change his life, and that there are far more benefits than drawbacks, we might have a chance to bond the father more permanently to his children.*

* *As a society we need to see that there is an evolutionary need for an active and present father as well as mother.*

* *The father can compliment the mothering by fathering his children. The two are needed to create full and whole children.*

* *This applies not just during the early years, but throughout the lives of the children.*

* *The father needs to see his input is valuable and of worth.*

* *Most important within the framework of the training we run for social worker is the concept that the father needs to realize that it is his time that is important for his children, not necessarily his money.*

* *The quality of shared time between a father and a child will determine a great many factors in the future development of the child.*

* *The children need more than just a father; they need other male role models, and one of the most important is the role of grandfather.*

141

SUGGESTIONS FOR ACTION
Couvade of the future

To create a new tradition of couvade would be very easy. We are moving towards it already.

* The potential father needs to be able to empathize with the mother-to-be. The Growth Chart I suggested in Chapter 6 is a good starting point. The father needs to know what is happening and how to support the mother through those changes.

* As the birth nears, the father should involve himself in all the pre-natal classes, and seek to be present at the birth. The description of the Mexican couvade ritual encapsulates the loving and tender relationship at this vital moment. I would recommend that the midwife reads this example and assists in the preparation of the space and environment with the father and mother to ensure something like this happens. The space into which the baby is born is of vital importance, and the father can involve himself in it's preparation.

* Once the baby is born, the father needs to bond with it as well as the mother. The placing of the baby onto his bare chest is very important, and needs to be done as soon as possible. The smell of the father should be imparted to the baby.

* The father should be involved in all big decisions and included in all aspects of the baby's life, and the taking of paternity leave is essential for this.

* Many young families are now much more open to job and work change. With the recession, the mother can be going back out and working and the father remaining at home – not a bad thing! Flexibility in parenting is the key, and the father is just as capable of caring and nurturing as the mother.

* Discussion and time together is such an important element as well. The mother and father need to bond again with each other.

Birth is natural

The birth of a baby is a one-off event. It is wonderful; it can be miraculous. To deny the father his presence and full participation in such a unique event is absurd. The birth of your child is a transformative process for both mother and father; it marks a stepping off point into a new way of being. Michel Odent, a leading British obstetrician, is quoted as saying that 'there is little good to come for either sex from having a man at the birth of a child'. This view not only lacks consideration for the natural process that is birth but it also disregards the future developmental needs of the child. His comes from the viewpoint of the professionals involved in hospital births. Basically, it would be much more convenient for them if the father wasn't present and potentially interfering. The natural conclusion of such a view is that the conscious participation of the mother is also a hindrance, so why not give her a general anaesthetic, and just perform caesareans all the time? This seems to be the way we are going with birth. We need to remember that birth is natural. We go to hospitals when we are ill or sick, and the mother is neither of these things. The more births which can take place at home or in similar places the better. Obviously, there is a need for some births to take place in hospital, but more effort needs to be made in this area.

The father leads by example, he takes on responsibility, he steps towards holistic experiences, he has emotions, he feels vulnerable, as well as being the leader and guide. This is the natural state of a man, whether he has children or not, he is a powerful and vulnerable being. He does the internal as well as the external work. He can be firm as well as soft. He attempts to balance the responsibility with his ability to continue to learn.

Good luck with all that then!

11

Rite of passage
Recognition

The Lesson
Give it away

The Age
Grandfather

West

The colour of **Blue**
Tranquillity and depth

144

THE SIXTH AGE
Grandfather

We cannot simply think of our survival; each new generation is responsible to ensure the survival of the seventh generation. The prophecy given to us, tells us that what we do today will affect the seventh generation and because of this we must bear in mind our responsibility to them today and always.
Our responsibility to the seventh generation
International Institute for Sustainable Development, 1992

The boy seeks to find himself, the father seeks to care for his immediate family. Possibly for the first time, when the man becomes a grandfather, he looks up and sees the bigger picture. The grandfather sees grandchildren, he sees the wider community, and he also sees his own vulnerability, his ageing, his slowing down. In this sense he is looking in two directions – back at his past life and forward to the future and things to come. To be a grandfather is to broaden our horizons.

THE RITE OF PASSAGE
Recognition
Separation - *He doesn't have to accumulate, he slows down*
Transition - *He starts to give things away, he teaches*
Incorporation - *He is recognized by others*
The father cares and shares with and for his family. His focus is still pretty small and self-centred. With the coming of the sixth age,

grandfather, we see a change – the development of a wider perspective, sharing beyond the immediate family and teaching outside the close circle. This comes about with the increase in leisure time which enables us to multi-task, not be so fixed. When we increase our leisure time, we don't decline, we actually expand. The grandfather becomes of value and use to his tribe, not just his family. He steps up to a new kind of responsibility and this is a very welcome and beautiful phase. He becomes visible to the wider world beyond his immediate family.

Beyond stability

The father builds, becomes, creates and maintains. We are talking on many levels – metaphysical as well as physical. Within this stability, the new growth (the baby) he has created is able to develop. This applies to a child, or equally to a business. Many men who do not have children nurture and protect their businesses in the same way as a father does his child. Indeed, nowadays, a lot of men nurture both, and many focus too intently on the business and neglect the child. However, we are hopefully dealing with a man who is in balance and can juggle such complex responsibilities. This period of stability, responsibility, and calm is essential. It can last for many years depending on the number of children, families, partners, businesses, etc. It's very valuable and very important work, but, like all ages, it inevitably comes to an end. For the father this is when his offspring leave home, for the businessman when his company becomes self-sustaining. We know we have reached this point when we receive recognition from beyond our immediate family. The grandfather is accepted into the wider community; he is recognized as being of value to his society. The rite of passage for grandfathers is recognition, and this operates on a number of levels.

Recognition internal and external

First, the recognition is internal. He recognizes he has achieved some of the things he set out to accomplish. He has been driven and focused, and by doing so he has now achieved, so he doesn't have to be so driven. Second, the recognition is external. He is recognized by others and he is now able to step into a position of authority. The community recognizes he has value and gifts. Often this means he becomes a teacher and shares his skills and knowledge with others. This rite is one of the easiest in that there are no hard tasks or challenges. This rite, unlike the previous ones, depends on others providing it for you. This rite is given to you by others; you can't claim it for yourself. In my case I was recently asked to become a visiting professor at Staffordshire University in recognition of my contribution to the field of community arts. It is a great honour and I feel very privileged to be offered such recognition. I am stepping towards being a grandfather, even though I don't have grandchildren yet.

Ageing

Some social gerontologists use the term 'young-old' for ages 55 to 74, and this roughly corresponds to what I call the 'grandfather' stage. The term 'old-old' is employed for ages 75 and beyond, and this is what I categorize as the 'elder' stage. However the aged are categorized, ageing is a highly individual experience. It is not a disease. It is, actually, a series of processes that begin with birth and continue throughout the life cycle. As individuals move through the processes, they become more and more different – physically, emotionally, intellectually – from everyone else. Thus, paradoxically, the ageing population is a very heterogeneous population. We differ more. What makes individuals as they age different from one another is a combination of many factors, for example, place of birth, place of residence, marital status, the foods eaten and not eaten, education, heredity, physical and mental health, family size and composition. The generation who fought in the Second World War have aged differently to those born after it. We are affected by our own time and place in history. Our experience of personal loss or grief, and our ability to mourn it or not, will affect our ageing process and resistance to illness. Because of the burgeoning size and heterogeneous nature of our ageing population, there is a rapidly increasing need to understand the consequences of ageing. Where once it was unusual for families to have three living generations, now it is not unusual for them to have four. Many people experience full lives for two to four decades past 60 years of age. In fact, they are quite capable of enjoying life fully until the end of their lives. As with all of these ages, we are going to have to redefine and create anew how to be and how to cope with the process. As Satchel Paige remarked, 'Age is a question of mind over matter. If you don't mind, it doesn't matter.'

THE LESSON
Give it away
To paraphrase **Bo Philps**, there are three stages of man:
He believes in Father Christmas,
He doesn't believe in Father Christmas
He is Father Christmas!
As a young man we are trying to make our way in the world. As a father we find our way in the world and we make our mark. As a grandfather we slow down. The grandfather has no need to make any more marks. Those who are not grandfathers will still come to this understanding about life. If we take the example of the businessman, we can see how the archetypes used in this book apply to the development of a career. When we first start out in business we are very inexperienced and tender, and it is worthwhile experimenting and making mistakes (the young seedling stretching tentatively above the soil, having to compete and being battered by the weather). These mistakes enable us to specialize and to recognize those skills and businesses we are best at. This early experimentation allows us to find our niche. When we feel we have done enough of this, we can really put our foot down (the young plant, growing vigorously towards the light, competing with and outstripping its neighbours). This is a period of accumulation – the

increasing and expanding of the company – and leads to responsibility. Previously, we have just been looking after ourselves, but now we are employing people. The business increases and with expansion of the business comes the next stage of development – delegation and the sharing of responsibilities (the plant bearing fruit, flowers). The individual recognizes that the tasks involved are so complex they have to be shared, and he gives away parts of the responsibility (young seedlings start growing around the original plant). This is the next stage of natural development. When we observe natural growth patterns, we see the inevitable 'decline' as well as 'ascent'. We see the decline as negative, because we live in a youth-focused culture. However, the decline is actually a hugely restorative process for the individual; it is positive. It allows us time to reflect. We don't have to compete so hard anymore, and we can take our time.

Monumentalism and self-made men

At present, we have many examples of 'self-made' men out there – Richard Branson, Bill Gates, Alan Sugar, etc. These individuals have been held up to us all as success stories, and I'm sure they lead very fulfilled lives. They all rely heavily on their family, friends and employees to run their empires. They may have started on their own, but they employ thousands of people to do the work. Individually they identify themselves with their company and enterprise. This is fine when we are young, but it is not the behaviour of a wise elder. The obsessive accumulation of wealth, business and status is against nature, not with it. This obsessive behaviour ensures the businesses they have created will live after they die. The business becomes a monument to the individual. This is not the correct way to be. Human beings have not always lived this way, but we have to go back quite a while to reconnect to the principles of which I am talking. Archaeologists bemoan the lack of artefacts from our ancestors before the year 3000BC. In evolutionary terms, this is just in our recent past. There is very little evidence of any structures, monuments or buildings from before this time. We left just a few bones and some carvings. We can either say that is because we didn't have the tools and means to construct on a large scale, or I would argue, we chose not to. From about 3000BC onwards, all over the world we very conveniently began leaving huge monuments – Stonehenge, the Sphinx and pyramids, Machu Picchu, Ajanta in Satavahana and so many others. Monumentalism, for me, marked the departure from the natural cycle, and starts the decline of mankind. These monuments were continued through into the medieval churches and the skyscrapers of our modern age. When we seek to make huge marks and impressions on the world, then we are not becoming grandfathers or elders. We choose instead to step beyond the natural ways, to put ourselves above the cycle and web of life, and we create monuments to our stupidity and selfishness. We need to reconnect to the true meaning of becoming a grandfather.

Yoga of grandfathers

I ran a weekend with men working on the principles of the ages of men. During the course of the workshop we experienced as a group the essences of the ages. We struggled to express the essence of grandfather, because many of us were still young. Then, whilst doing some yoga exercises, I thought about creating the essence symbolically. So we stood with firmly planted feet and stretched out our left arm to 'accumulate', stretching it out and then drawing it back to our heart. At the same time, the right arm remained fixed, cocked across and out from the chest, creating a safe 'harbour' in which the accumulations could be stored. This was for me the essence of father. The fixed nature of the right arm caused discomfort after a while, and I realized this represented illness, stress, fatigue, all those symptoms of over-work we carry with us. So, in order to liberate and change the dynamic, we had to open out the right arm, stretching it out to the world. The left arm continued to accumulate, but the right arm gave it away. The synchronicity of the movement, drawing in and then letting go, became very poetic and balanced. If I fill my head with ideas, and retain them, not sharing them with others, then I become full, stagnant and have no room for new ideas. This is the present business development model. It doesn't allow us to clear out and refresh ourselves.

THE AGE
Grandfather
Development and decline
We all grow old, we cannot avoid this simple truth. As we age our senses change. The sharpness of our hearing starts to decline around the age of 50, and by 65 about 30% of all people have significant hearing impairment. Our eyes start to decline from the age of 30 onwards. By the time we are 60 our pupils decrease to about a third of the size they were when 20. Almost everyone over the age of 55 needs glasses at least part of the time. The number of taste buds decreases from the age of 40 in women and 50 in men. Our sense of smell diminishes significantly, especially after the age of 70. After the age of 50 many people have a reduced sensitivity to pain. For some us, our body weight grows. The accumulation of fat can increase and our ability to burn it off decreases. Sometimes our sexual potency decreases, or maybe our interest in it declines. Our brains remain as active as ever, and hopefully we keep on learning. Our senses may diminish, but our sense of who we are may well increase. One of the major changes in our approach to ageing should be the development of generational intelligence, as illustrated in the *Responsibility to the Seventh Generation* quoted at the beginning of this Chapter.

Within the archetype of the family, there is a huge difference between being a father and being a grandfather. Typically, grandparents say to me, 'It's so much better being a grandparent, you can look after the children for a day, and then you give them back to the parents when they get grouchy!' This is the essence of the age – the ability to be more relaxed, more at ease and not so fraught and caught up within the day-to-day. The grandfather enjoys life. Many fathers tell me, 'My dad is a far better grandfather than he was a father.' And so he should be! Grandfathers can afford to be relaxed. The grandfather is a real blessing on his family and on his wider community. This comes from his ability to teach. The grandfather passes on his skills and knowledge, and he distils knowledge into wisdom. For me this is a vital link in the chain of a healthy community. The lessons he has learnt during his time of accumulation and responsibility are passed on to the next generations. This happens particularly well between grandfather and grandchild. There is a mutual respect and connection so much simpler than the father/son relationship. I remember my parents coming to visit my young family, and watching as my father lay on the floor to play with my two young children. I struggled as tears came to my eyes as I remembered he had never played that way with me as a small child.

Teaching

The way in which the grandfather teaches is different from the father. The grandfather, having more time and not being so personally involved, is able to bring fun, joy and lightness to his teachings. Indeed, one very strong element of grandfather teaching is the idea that it is a two-way process. The grandson teaches the grandfather just as much as the other way around. The grandfather must be prepared to continue learning. Far too many men feel once they have reached a certain age the world can teach them nothing new. This is a terrible place to be. The know-it-all who starts every sentence with the phrase 'In my day it was different...' is not open to change or an admiration of the present. In such a confused place we are perpetuating the tyrant energy; we become bitter and resentful. The positive man continues to learn. I remember my own grandfather who was a wonderful example. My brother and I were supporters of QPR football club, and my grandfather had absolutely no interest in football. However, each week he would make himself read the sports columns and on the weekends when he visited he would be a fountain of knowledge on football. At the time I wasn't aware of his previous disinterest, and it is only with hindsight that I can admire such commitment.

Planning for the future

To continue the business analogy, the grandfather stage is when we don't take business so personally. We realize that the next generation can now take charge and move it into different areas. This can only happen if we give it away or we teach others. We have many names for this process – becoming a consultant, slowing down, down-sizing, changing gear. In the past we 'retired'. This caused a huge amount of trouble. From being active, involved and lively, the man suddenly felt useless and deprived of his purpose, and he often died very quickly on retirement, or, if he managed it well, learnt new skills and went on a cruise. Ceasing work shouldn't happen suddenly when we are 65. It needs to be worked on, planned and incorporated into our lives over a period of years. I have assisted many business people in moving from being fully active in their business to being employed part-time and combining this with voluntary work. Many older people are now choosing to 'put something back' into society as they age, and I have just assisted a CEO in setting up a two year sabbatical with Voluntary Service Overseas in Malaysia, where he will be able to help indigenous people to set up localized farming communes.

Growing bitter

A great many businesspeople identify so strongly with their companies and businesses that they are unable to let go, and when they do retire or have to quit due to ill health, they become bitter and depressed. My father was an example of this. He was a political journalist for over 30 years, and he mastered this highly competitive and very specialized field.

However, as he approached retirement and stepped outside his field, he noticed that his friends and work colleagues promptly dropped him. They didn't contact him, and he became old news very quickly. The lessons he had learnt were not passed on, and the next generation failed to learn from his example. This is so typical of a competitive market, and my father grew bitter and resentful as he went deeper into retirement. The first thing he would say to me when I came to visit was, 'Have you got a job yet?' He thought working long hours and being in a trade was essential. My own way of working, being self-employed and reliant on part-time work means I have been in semi-retirement for a long time already!

The Indian concept of sannyasa sums up the idea of grandfatherhood. According to the *Bhagavad Gita*: '*The giving up of activities that are based on material desire is what great learned men call the renounced order of life [sannyasa]. And giving up the results of all activities is what the wise call renunciation [tyaga].*' (18.2) Maharishi Mahesh Yogi's translation of verse 3, chapter 5 of the *Bhagavad-Gita* says: '*Know him to be ever a man of renunciation who neither hates nor desires; free from the pairs of opposites, he is easily released from bondage, O mighty-armed.*' This reinforces the idea of a two-fold process: the giving up of material goods, which I am calling 'the giveaway', and then the renunciation, which I will develop within the next age, eldership. We need to learn the ways of being young-old, before we can become old-old.

Mid-life crisis

As grandparents we have the time to reflect on life and such thoughts can lead to what is known as the mid-life crisis, which is just an expression of frustration about the compromises we have made. There are many men at the grandfather age who have gone out and bought a motorbike or a flashy red sports car, and these represent their last chance to pursue their ascent into maleness. At the same time some men have affairs with younger women, and this represents their wish to remain young and virile. I can understand such sentiments and actions, and nowadays many more women are behaving this way as well as men. The need to act so impulsively may be borne out of frustration at the amount of times they have had to act sensibly whilst being a father. The extent of this mid-life rebellion can differ between men, depending on the level of satisfaction they have gained from their lives. Those who have pursued their soul's purpose and found it are far less likely to need this last fling.

By having fulfilled a lot of your needs, by having helped others and by being able to see how you have made important contributions to others lives, you may reached a gentle place of reflection. However, this will not be the case if you feel you have missed out on opportunities and that you haven't done the things you really wanted to do, or you feel resentful about the way in which others have restricted your growth. The latter reflection can lead to radical action in mid-life, and this in turn can lead to many changes – relationships, work, residence, etc. If we are able to resist breaking the relationship with out other half at this point, then later life can be a very wonderful joint adventure. With the children leaving home, the husband and wife can redefine and find each other. They can leave the house, go travelling and explore the world. This is a wonderful time, and one of the benefits of being grandparents.

THE PAST

The *Xiao Jing*, written around 470BC, includes a conversation between Confucius and his student Zen Shen. In the discussion Confucius sets out how to create a worthwhile community, and one of the most important principles is that of 'filial piety'. The concept is broken down into duties:
To take care of one's parents
To engage in good conduct inside and outside the home
To perform duties that ensure the material means to support your parents

To show love and respect, and not to rebel
To ensure male heirs
To wisely advise one's parents
To display sorrow for their sickness and death
To carry out sacrifices after their death
During the Han Dynasty, those who neglected their 'filial piety' could receive corporal punishment. I don't think we need a return to filial piety, but the younger generations should respect the older ones. On their part, however, the parents ought to earn respect through action and example. Just because we reach a certain age doesn't mean we automatically gain respect.

While we deserve respect and attention from our children, we also don't want to be a burden on them as we age. With the introduction of Buddhism to China came a different attitude, and the *Mouzi Lihuolun* illustrates this. The Buddhist belief was to encourage the older men to leave their families, and by doing so overcome the sorrow and grief which are 'born of those who are dear.' Whereas the previous system encouraged loyalty and support, the Buddhist individual was expected to seek salvation by severing links to the family. These two different beliefs sum up the two stages of being old – the young-old is revered and of value to his community, while the elder or old-old steps away from his commitments and responsibilities, and becomes more reclusive.

Grandparents are teachers

In all indigenous cultures the grandparents played vital roles in the education of the grandchildren. Almost invariably most children were taught by their grandparents, not by their parents. This reflected the 'extended' nature of tribal life. When a family lives in a compound, not a house, then the grandparents live within the compound of their children and grandchildren. In return for this provision the grandparents teach and care for the children, whilst the parents are out collecting food or doing the work. This was a simple and readily recognized way of living, and it suited everyone.

THE PRESENT

With the development of square houses and the concept of a 'nuclear family' – two parents and 2.4 children – the grandparents were somewhat forgotten. In Western Europe it was only in the late-17th and 18th centuries that the nuclear family became dominant, and on the other continents it was a much more recent phenomenon. The development of the nuclear family was only ever due to its economic viability; it provided none of the obvious other social and educational benefits of the extended family for children, parents and grandparents. The extended family has become a rarity in this age, and this reflects our reliance on money and capitalism more than the non-viability of the extended family per se. Indeed, if we were to take into consideration the present costs of child-care and education for most families where both parents are working, we would probably find that the extended family is the more economically viable. In the meantime the grandparents have sought alternatives.

Old people ghettos

To a large extent we have ghettoized our old people. Large numbers of elderly British people have set up communities in Spain, created an idealized and weird combination of fish and chips, warm beer and perpetual sunshine. Safe within these ghettos they moan and complain about foreigners coming to Britain and ruining the place, never once contemplating that they might be doing the same to Spain! These isolated communities perpetuate and exaggerate racial prejudices and fears. This is not how young-old people should behave. They should be actively involved in their grandchildren's lives, and continue to learn. Such ghettos are built on the perpetuation of wealth and accumulation of material things; they run contrary to the idea of the giveaway. Our old people are taught and encouraged to be selfish rather than sharing. In recent years we have been subjected to a television programme called *Grumpy Old Men,* simple interviews with young-old men who spend the whole time bemoaning the injustices and perceived declines in British life. What a missed opportunity, despite the humour and self-effacement of the programme. Why couldn't they have made a programme called *Wise Old Men?* In which these same people encouraged youngsters with tales of daring deeds and inspired us all with the wisdom and knowledge gained through experience and mistakes. That would be the proper way of giving away, and a step toward a positive and respectful view of being a grandfather.

THE FUTURE

Our Members of Parliament have an average age of about 49 years; 14% are under 40, 18% over 60, and 68% between 41 and 59 – for me this is very young. Despite all recent troubles in terms of expense accounts and integrity, the idea of being an elected Member of Parliament does and should reflect a certain amount of responsibility and respect. The real meaning of the job is one of being in a vocation, of service to your community, of being the grandfather-figure. It should not be about trying to find and make your mark in the world, like the father. We have too many fathers in parliament, and not enough grandfathers. A young-old person, who has given away and has stopped taking things so personally, would be ideal as a Member of Parliament. He would be able to serve his community without his personal issues and needs getting in the way. This means he would still be trying to learn and still be prepared to be flexible and adaptable. I would advocate at least 50% of them being women as well.

I am seeking to reinstate the grandfather as the really cool and worthwhile person to be. Grandfathers once involved themselves in their grandchildren's lives in a very positive and useful way. Due to our increased fears around paedophilia the input of older men into young children's lives has been stunted. This is a tragedy, not only for the grandfathers, but most especially for the children.

SUGGESTIONS FOR ACTION
Intergenerational projects
I was involved in a pilot project in a small community up the Rhondda Valley in South Wales. We gave the 9 to 11 year old children a basic training in how to listen and express themselves through creativity. They were then introduced to a nearby care home for the elderly, and individually they were paired with an old person to record and document their stories. The care workers for the elderly were stunned by the depth, quality and detail of the stories told. Frequently, old people who had been reticent, quiet and introverted became animated, talkative and smiled in the company of the young children. We are now reversing the process, and about to undertake a training programme for elderly people to go into schools and participate in the classrooms as teachers' assistants, and also as learners. Such projects always show how old and young people benefit in a variety of ways through being in each other's company. These schemes are very simple to introduce and the educational benefits for the children are very interesting. After the first project we asked the class what professions they would choose in later life, and over 40% said they would consider being a carer. Most didn't even know what that meant before the project started.

Integrated communities
In the last year I have been involved in the embryonic stages of a community in the West of England. The community will be mostly older people in small units, but will also deliberately integrate single-parent families. The intention is to allow the older people to support and encourage the single mothers and fathers. The community is also seeking links to a local school and the development of a mutual support system

between the age groups, the youngsters teaching the older people how to use the internet, etc. I'm encouraged that such initiatives are seeking to allow older people to have a positive and respectful input into the wider community. They are a fantastic resource and need to be used wisely.

12

Rite of passage
Supervising bravery

The Lesson
Forgiveness

The Age
Elder

North West

The colour of **Green**
Nature, at peace

THE SEVENTH AGE
Elder

Despite all the ghastliness that is around, human beings are made for goodness. The ones who ought to be held in high regard are not the ones who are militarily powerful, nor even economically prosperous. They are the ones who have a commitment to try and make the world a better place. We – The Elders – will endeavour to support those people and do our best for humanity.
Desmond Tutu

THE RITE OF PASSAGE
Supervising bravery
Separation - *He steps away from the family*
Transition - *He holds teenagers through their rite of passage*
Incorporation - *He forgives*

Eldership is a state of mind, not a result of ageing. Elders attain a state of being which transcends their material needs and the psychological desires. They are able to make judgments taking into consideration the needs of others, and they base their actions on a commitment to love. This is an advanced state of being, and one that we should seek to attain. Before I go much further I need to say I am slightly wary of this chapter, as I am talking about concepts I have not experienced within my own life. However, I know the essence of the concepts can be experienced by all of us during our lives at given times. The child can be the elder in moments of need, just as a grandfather can behave like a baby! I also know these next chapters are aspirations of mine, and for that reason alone they are of value and worth sharing.

Worth to his community

Building on the previous chapter about grandfathers, I would like to develop the concept of the grandfather truly being recognized as having given away. Throughout his life thus far the grandfather has taken from his community; it has supported and encouraged him. Without others he would not have made it. To show his appreciation for all this support, he now needs to give back to the community, and he does this through the supervision of the teenagers. This was a widespread phenomenon in all the continents of the world throughout history, and remnants of it survive to this day. The grandfather's rite of passage is the supervision of the teenage rites of passage. As we said in the previous chapter, this process reflected the increase in time and leisure the grandfather possesses, and was a very natural event. In all cultures this was seen as the grandfather proving his worth. He supervised a young man not from his family. In this way he began to receive recognition and became a trusted figure in the wider community, not just his immediate family. This was a hugely important rite. It was the culmination of the man's life thus far. The elders taught the teenagers, the community gave back to the elders, the teenagers grew, the elders grew – everyone was a winner!

Supervising teenagers

If we were to allow our grandfathers to work directly with our teenagers, initiating and encouraging them to become men, we would transform our present social troubles. The elders need to create appropriate rites of passage for the teenagers. In Chapter 9 I described the rite for teenagers in the Samburu tribe. This would not be appropriate here in Britain, but the principle remains true. Teenagers

163

need guidance, and their grandfathers can provide it, by encouraging the teenagers to live life to the full. The teenager stands at the foot of a high mountain pass, and wants to find his way through the treacherous terrain. He should seek the advice of a guide who has been up and down the mountain many times over the person who has never been there before. The teenager should turn to the elder, not his peer, for guidance. It doesn't make the journey any less dangerous, but it does mean he is with someone who knows where he is going.

Elders are confident

We need to acknowledge what we have learnt and been taught throughout our lives, and to then offer it to others. I work with an organization called the Circle of Life Rediscovery, and they organize and facilitate outdoor camping experiences for teenagers. I work for them because I know what I am doing. The organisation recognizes having a strong and confident male as part of their team is vital. Through the years of facilitating this work, they have employed, and had as volunteers, many older people. It is always fascinating to see how suitable they are. Many have never worked with teenagers, and, before they start, think it will be a simple task. Almost inevitably, however, they are challenged, and have to start dealing with their own past because of the behaviour of the teens. Additionally they have to deal with the conditions of working in a forest, under canvas, sometimes in the continual pouring rain for days on end. Many self-assured and confident old people leave as timid wrecks and never come back again.   This is because, however experienced they may be, they have not consciously been through the processes of rites of passage themselves. They may well have done lots of activities and had many good experiences. These young-old people are attracted to the work because they need to do the work for themselves. Unfortunately, we are not facilitating the process for them – it is for the teenagers. Many come and want to join in the sweat lodge or other activities being offered, and we have to gently dissuade them. An elder will have done the work, and must now prepared to share it with the teenagers, not try to experience it himself.

THE LESSON
Forgiveness

Grandfather Buzzard

I live on the air
The air supports me in my flight
I adjust my feathers, minutely, with care.
When I want to take off
I have to open my chest
I have to open my chest to spread my wings
When I do this all my wounds are rent open.
All the wounds in my body expand.
In that expansion
The internal light shines through the wounds
The light within is allowed out.
Only by opening my chest can it shine.
By doing so, I show who I really am
My true identity is revealed
My wounds proclaim my beauty.
My wounds, my hurt, my sorrow, shine out as I fly.
They illuminate the world as I fly above it
I claim my place in the universe by being open-chested
By risking to show my wounds in their true light.

Again, one of the series of shamanic journeys I undertook with First Nations teachers, this is an archetypal lesson about life. The buzzard is teaching us a simple lesson: the wounds we receive can either be thought of as a hindrance or a blessing. By risking showing his wounds he becomes a blessing to the world. This surely leads us to forgiveness. Forgiveness is the key to success at being an elder. All too often I come across older people who bemoan the lack of respect that young people show them. You do not earn respect by simply being 60 years old; you earn it by being authentic. If you are a miserable old git, then you will be treated as such. To stop moaning and complaining about life means we are content with our lot. To be content is to accept our wounds and losses as well as our triumphs and wonders. When we reach contentment our vitality increases and we are respected. In order to achieve all this, we need to forgive ourselves.

Transcending guilt and shame

The elder has been through the process of examining his life and sorting out all the events and experiences. In that examination of the past he identified the huge amount of guilt and blame given to him by his parents, siblings and friends, and the ways in which these have been internalized. We all accumulate guilt and shame; we are brilliant at accumulating them. As with material goods, they mean nothing in the end. When we come to examine such accumulations correctly we identify the root of guilt as being misunderstanding. All guilt starts with a misunderstanding and misrepresentation of the truth. If we can see this we can transform the guilt and let it go, and by doing so come into the moment. When we do this we dissipate the amount of fear in the future. So an elder is in the process of letting go of his guilt about the past and decreasing the fear of the future. At present, we encourage our old people to retain their guilt, and they exponentially increase their fear for the future. Forgiveness of ourselves is the key to understanding our relationships with others; it enables us to forgive them as well. The Samurai death ritual involved the forgiveness of others in preparation for battle. Interestingly, this meant the forgiveness of all the warrior's enemies, as well as the completion of all unfinished business and the letting go of debts, grudges, guilt and anger. By finishing all the angry business the warriors could fight to the death beautifully!

Relationship

As I said in the last chapter, this is the time in which the long-term relationship can blossom and become a true blessing on the world. To be in the company of two elderly people who love and care for each other is to be blessed. Their sharing is not like young people; there is a sense of permanence and trust, which can only be gained with time. Elders can transform us not just through teaching us by words or deeds; we are transformed by spending time with them. They are not trying to teach lessons; they *are* the lessons. There was an older man who lived near my house, and he was a master craftsman, a maker of musical instruments. I would often find myself at his workshop in the afternoon, somehow gravitated to that place. There I would be watching him, sharing a cup of tea, telling him my troubles. Without intentionally going there, I would be drawn, and on returning (to my home) I would be refreshed and invigorated.

THE AGE

Elder

The old-old person is beyond caring about his senses and their deterioration. He is a mature and initiated man who loves life, has made many mistakes and has asked questions. His journey has been varied, diverse and beautiful, and he is now entering his last years, conscious of the proximity of death. Elders need to be brave again, to step towards the unknown, to be positive. The Yin and Yang of eldership is the combination of the two opposing states of being – life and death – enabling the two to dance together, to be present, and in their dance to create the third state of being: conscious, aware, non-judgmental and at peace.

Eldership

I am not an elder yet, but I have inklings as to how they might behave and what they might offer teenagers:

* An elder facilitates an experience for others, and receives the rewards in a variety of subtle ways. The rewards are in the witnessing of moments of revelation for the teenagers, and that is sufficient. The teenagers either get it or don't, and you can never tell beforehand when the lesson will be learnt or what the lesson will be. The elder doesn't take the process personally, doesn't say, 'I made that happen.' This would spoil the moment, and cheat the teenager of the experience.

* An elder doesn't have to force or bully a teenager into an experience. A true elder is so attractive and interesting to teenagers, and to the rest of his community, that he develops respect and trust instantly in those around him. He doesn't have to operate in the ways which younger people do. I try to teach this behaviour to men who work with teenagers, but it doesn't come naturally to them. A lot of men who work with teenagers want to show off, want to be seen, want to teach and be visible. I show them how to just 'be', to act as if they are at home, without showing off or drawing attention to themselves. This means the individuals come to them of their own volition; the teenagers come out of curiosity, to learn by example and by choice.

Before we can teach we need to have been initiated ourselves, and that is why I now run eldership-training programmes. On these I enable older people to retrospectively put themselves through rites, and catch up with themselves. I will talk a little more about these at the end of this chapter. Elders are the ones who can make light of the darkest situations, because they have been there themselves. They are the ones who have the depth of experience to knock the cockiness out of brash teenagers. They are not like the boys' fathers; they are of the grandfathers' age. The importance of this age difference has been known about since time immemorial.

168

Examples of elders

I used to work with an ex-sailor and soldier, Jack Sullivan, who passed away a few years ago, blessed be his memory. He would come with me to some of the very troubled schools, and would sit at the back watching proceedings. He would observe and help the children to draw, as he loved drawing. In one troubled classroom he stepped forward and accosted one of the teenagers who was particularly aggressive.

'So, you're a gangster are you?' Jack asked.

'Yeah, I'm scary, dangerous and hard,' came the glib reply.

'Have you ever killed anyone?' Jack asked with a wry smile on his face.

'Well . . . no . . . but, you know,' came the slightly deflated reply.

'I have,' said Jack quietly.

At the end of the lesson this untouchable, hardened boy was literally sitting on Jack's lap; he had regressed to being a six year old. If he'd been able to suck his thumb, he would have.

'Please, Jack, tell me another story.'

Jack had tamed a complete tearaway in less than an hour. I couldn't do it, I was just in my 30s; and I still haven't killed anyone!

I frequently take older men into the schools with me. I took a group of retired coal miners into a school in Nantyglo, down the South Wales Valleys. They sat conspiratorially in the back row of the class as I worked on an environmental project. At the end of the lesson the teenage boys came up to me. One said, 'Those old boys were disgusting,' a genuine look of bewilderment on his face. 'They know all about SEX,' he gasped. He'd never thought older people would be like that.

Elders move towards death

Older men can do a job the mother, the father and women can't do. They can confront teenagers with the truth. They know what the teenagers are going through, and they can support them in creative and imaginative ways, ways the parents can't even conceive of. They should be full of life, mischief and adventure – not moaning old gits sitting at home complaining about the world. The older men need to know what it is to have lived, and they need to be able to encourage their young charges to be adventurous too.

An elder has been through the period of accumulation, and is in the process of letting it go. He doesn't want the clutter of his previous life, and he is simplifying. This simplification process is the next phase of human evolution, summed up in that wonderful phrase, 'You can't take it with you.' Just as the initiate boy walks towards pain, the necessary pain of initiation into manhood, an elder walks towards death, the inevitable ending of his days which we all have coming. When he walks towards it willingly, he is free, liberated from the everyday concerns previously so important to him. He is able to be as childish as he likes, or as serious, it doesn't matter. A boy becoming a man is an initiate, and a grandfather becoming an elder is an initiate too. All initiates accept the pain of initiation as a gift to their ancestors, and it is their hope that it will liberate them into the next phase of life. We used to be well versed in the inevitability of our life and death. We lived with death as an everyday occurrence; we saw it face to face when we killed for our food. We were also more in tune with the changing and passing of the seasons, the influence of decay and compost. We seem to have lost the memory of this contact with the earth – temporarily, I hope – and we seem afraid to grow old.

Change happens

When a boy wants to become a teenager, he accepts the inevitable pain of initiation as something to be tolerated before he can become a man. It is inevitable that your children will leave home, and you will not need to have the same physical or material goods. We are all moving in the same direction and you cannot stand still or turn back time. When we resist and try to fight against this, we create fear, illness, pain and stress. If we fear the inevitable, we extend our inability to accept our fate. By remaining uninitiated, immature and without hope, we create more fear. A true elder has been initiated into manhood and initiated into eldership, and in the end he will be initiated into death. In the West we cling to life; our old people have their lives extended into pain, inaction, fear, despair, loneliness, confusion and anger. Hospitals and medicines prolonging misery and illness. This isn't eldership. It's an uninitiated extension of childhood, promoted by fear.

Knowledge becomes wisdom

An elder needs to breath death and life. He needs to be at ease with sacrifice, and the passing of the seasons. He needs to know about all of this, and to have experienced it all many times. Such an individual is not only unafraid of teenagers, he is not afraid of anyone! If he hasn't started to learn these lessons then he can't teach the younger generations; he will be too similar to them. He will have no wisdom to impart, so he will only pass on knowledge. Many older people have experienced a great deal and made a 'success' of their lives. That is fine, but it doesn't mean they can inevitably teach teenagers. To teach them you have to have processed life internally, asked questions of yourself and faced the answers, however tough they might be. The distillation of knowledge into wisdom is not simple. Wisdom needs to be imparted in very specific ways: without attachment, with as little ego as possible, whilst encouraging personal exploration and supporting individual growth, independent of reliance on the teacher. Although describing a practitioner-patient relationship, I think the following sums up this part of eldership beautifully: *'As the earth is indifferent to the seed, so the practitioner is working with indifference towards the ailments or difficulties of the patient. Indifference here means one without difference or inclination, not inclined to prefer one thing to another, neutral. The driving force behind this commitment is passion for life. So, the practitioner, knowing that he is compassion, shares his own passion for life with the passion for life within the* *patient.'*[14]*   An elder doesn't turn a teenager away from a potential mistake, as the parent would. The elder knows that the lessons come in the mistakes, and this makes him unpopular. One of the most striking features of the elders I've worked with all over the world is the fact that they do not need you to like them. They know who they are, they are content and if you want to befriend them then you are welcome to try, but very unlikely to succeed!

THE PAST

In the past elders supervised teenagers, and by doing so, they were recognised as being of value to their community. Once the rite was completed these old-old people then carried on their lives. We really do not know how long prehistoric people lived. Anthropologists cannot give us the information as the remains with which they deal are just tantalizing fragments. If the Bible is to be believed, the early humans - Adam, Seth, Enoch – lived for more than 900 years. I'm not sure that I agree. After the populations began to increase, our life spans decreased to only 200 years, and by the time of King David (circa 1000BC), 70 years was a good age. I think we can all agree that from this point on there was a steep decline, and by medieval times the average life expectancy was about 30 years. In 1840 the life expectancy of a Swedish woman was 45 years, and yet by 2000, Japanese women had a life expectancy of 85 years. Right now the average life expectancy for the humans on the planet is 66; it is this low due to the devastating effects of AIDS and other ecological disasters. In Britain the average life expectancy is 78 – women 81 and men 76. On the whole the average life expectancy is on the increase and is showing no signs of topping out. Maybe we are moving back towards our past longevity... who knows?

THE PRESENT
Young youth workers
In order for our boys to pass through being teenagers and become men, we need elders to supervise their rites. Our teenagers need a good range of role models and midwives to help them through their troubled times. By doing this work properly, we create wholesome and vibrant communities. However, these elders have to know what is suitable and useful for these teenagers, and how to initiate them.

At present, we employ youth and social workers and teachers to do this complex work. How can a youth worker offer the kinds of rites of passage these young people desperately need, when he or she hasn't been initiated? The great majority of youth and community workers are in their 20s and 30s, and to be honest, because they are not elders, many cannot do this work properly. I know it may sound as though I am being dismissive of youth and community workers, but I am not. I am just saying that young ones are not necessarily good ones. I have worked in many community and youth centres in a wide range of settings. Indeed, when I started doing this work I was 19 myself, and I worked in a residential children's home. I was in charge of children up to the age of 18, and the closeness of our ages was problematic on occasions. Many times I was confronted by semi-naked or naked girls attempting to lure me into their rooms, and the frequency of affairs between the staff and youths paid testimony to the difficulty of such intense work. We need appropriate elders.

THE FUTURE
Elder training
Government departments, local authorities and charitable trusts all ask me the same question.
'What should we do with young people?'

173

My answer is almost invariably baffling to them.
'Release the elders from their enclaves.'

To initiate young men into adulthood we need older men. Right now we have an ageing population so we have a huge resource available for this job. We are not using them at all in this context, or in so many other ways. The majority of older people are living away from young people. Many of them would be ideal for the job, but a large percentage would need training before I would let them loose with teenagers, mainly because they have learnt to be bitter and scornful, and this is not useful or conducive to unconditional positive regard. The rather longer answer to the question is to put teenagers through community led rites of passage run by elders who have been appropriately trained. Without the appropriate elders in place, any rites of passage will be flimsy and worthless. So the first step must be towards retrospective rites of passage for elders. You can't put a teenager through something you haven't experienced yourself. These elders need to be in their 40s, 50s or 60s and need to be able to see the value and worth of such work. Form an orderly queue here please.

I am presently starting a training programme for older people based on the qualities I believe are needed in an elder who can work with teenagers. To be prescriptive is not particularly helpful, but here are some examples:
* *To be optimistic about life, and about the future*
* *To be wicked, mischievous*
* *To seek to learn at all times*
* *To seek the humorous or weird*
* *To be assured and confident in their identity*
* *To not be racially prejudiced, to not believe the media, to not think 'they're all over here taking away our jobs,' to understand the importance of racial integration*

174

* To be able to listen and not jump in
* To have been disappointed, to have made mistakes

The concept of 'eldership' and the idea that we should support and promote older people seems to be coming to the fore around the world. A new development, *The Elders*, includes some very wise and wonderful people as ambassadors for change. I quote from their manifesto:
'*The Elders can speak freely and boldly, working both publicly and behind the scenes. They will reach out to those who most need their help. They will support courage where there is fear, foster agreement where there is conflict and inspire hope where there is despair.*' **Nelson Mandela.**
* *The Elders amplify the voices of those who work hard to be heard, challenge injustice, stimulate dialogue and debate and help others to work for positive change in their societies.*
* *The Elders do not hold public office and have no political or legislative power. Because they are not bound by the interests of any single nation, government or institution, they are free to speak boldly and with whomever they choose on any issue, and to take any action that they believe is right.*
* *When undertaking initiatives, the Elders are committed to listening to the views of all groups and individuals – and especially women and young people. The Elders work both publicly and behind the scenes and at all levels - local, national and international - lending support and advice when invited, and sometimes when it is not.*

Now that's what we need more of.

SUGGESTIONS FOR ACTION
The wizard's apprentice
In one primary school I had been asked to visit, the teachers had been preparing the children by showing them pictures of the work I had done elsewhere. We were all going to make a mosaic mural. This was the first time they'd ever had an artist come to work with them, so everyone was

very excited. On the morning of my first day, I came in the classroom, and sat whilst the children were registering; they cast furtive glances towards me throughout the time. Eventually, the teacher gathered them together, and asked:

'So, this is Nick, what does he do?'

A young lad was closely scrutinizing me, taking in my white pointy beard, my green sweater, my arm full of colourful bracelets. He put his hand up. 'He's a wizard,' he stated firmly. I concurred, and we all laughed.

As you will have realized by now, I work in a wide range of settings with a wide range of people, and I have a great working life. Over the last 10 years of so, I have been self-employed, and yet during this time I have almost always had a young man working alongside me in some capacity or other. I should think there have been about 5 or 6 in this period. I don't know how they find me. I don't advertise or promote the opportunity. They just appear. They become my apprentice for a year or sometimes longer. Then they go off and do other things. The work I do attracts a certain kind of person. They come to me to be taught or just to hang out with me. Recently, I had a lad who was 22 who would come and dig my garden with me in return for me teaching him some basic shamanic practices. I am open to the opportunities and lessons that occur within these times, so they keep coming. Apprenticeships do not have to be strict or rigid; they can also be just about spending time together, and appreciating each other's company. Often the boys want to be recognized, acknowledged and listened to. It's as simple as that.

Retrospective rites for older people

Whilst organizing and participating in men's groups I often come across individuals who are seeking ritual and ceremony. They feel it is lacking in their lives, and once they have participated in one, they realize how restorative and powerful they can be. In order to explain how this works I'll give an example of a retrospective ceremony created over a three-day period in 1999. My wife and I facilitated about 40 people in the process, but, as with all such events, both of us learned and gained from the experience as well. The participants were an equal mix of men and women, and they ranged from their early 20s through to 60s. Some were parents, all were children, and we wanted to retrospectively take them through the experience of being blessed and honoured by their parents. We are all children, and we all need to be honoured by our parents, but for many of us this doesn't happen for a wide range of reasons. It is still possible to do this work retrospectively, and the men and women took it in turns to represent 'mother' and 'father', and each became the child as well. The rituals were designed by the groups. They were unique, formed out of the ether, out of our desires and collective needs. It was a co-creative process ensuring everyone felt part of the overall ceremony.

The men met separately from the women, and we created our rituals independently, coming together on the final day to complete the process. Amazingly, the rituals turned out to be almost exact mirror images of each other, even though Manda and I had not discussed our separate formats. The men were blessed as 'sons' by the 'mothers' first; and then the women were blessed as 'daughters' by the 'fathers'. As with all rituals, in amongst the physical structures and frameworks there were running, crying and playing young children, teenagers, parents and grandparents, onlookers and participants. Co-creation, retrospective ritual and blessing, we had the lot! Within the men's group I was acting in the Grandfather role, stepping back, taking in and keeping hold of the bigger picture, gently encouraging from the side-line and holding the trust in the process of the ritual. Co-creation allows all those participating to feel valued and honoured, for everyone to gain a sense of ownership and pride from the ceremony.

Shared grief

For the men, the first task was to let go of the grief stored up in them from their individual life journeys and from within their DNA. They had to tell their stories, tell of the pain, cry and let out all the deeply rooted anguish. I placed a large rock crystal in the centre of the circle as a focus and 'container' for the grief. It was really simple, as these things are when it comes down to it. The men were encouraged to direct their grief into that stone, whose nature is to hold. It formed a real and solid core to the process. This kind of grief is passed down the line by generations who have not been able to grieve in this way. It is the stuff of world wars, of poverty, of lost loves and physical hardship. We may be carrying this simply through our family name, or in the historical limitations that have shaped us as individuals. This grief turns naturally to praise once it has been dealt with, and the men were able to praise and honour their relations as part of the ritual. They came to that place of their own accord, but only after a great deal of grief.

Blessing their daughters

Having liberated themselves, the men were ready and capable of releasing their daughters into their independent lives, away from the father. Many men didn't have daughters, but were able to do the work very well. The women of all ages went through the following series of stages in which they were retrospectively honoured:
• *Unconditional love – welcoming and honouring the daughter, blessing her nature without condition or prejudice.*
• *Hearing her dreams – allowing her to state her vision, and then honouring and blessing it.*
• *Holding her, either physically, if requested, or by standing next to her – to enable the daughter to know she has been held.*
• *Blessing her outward journey – giving her a little bundle of wisdom and food for the journey, and reminding her that she takes a part of her father with her, wherever she goes.*

These four stages were manned by different individuals who spent a long time preparing both mentally and psychologically for the task. They undertook it with gusto and real conviction. Many women broke down and cried through each stage. There was no hurrying or forcing, and the women took hours to pass through all the stages. This was a very moving and cathartic experience for all involved, and was a huge blessing on those who participated and those watching. The participants felt they had retrospectively been welcomed and encouraged out into the wide world with love and honour by their fathers – even if they didn't know their fathers, or the father was deceased. It healed a great many wounded hearts and souls. It is never too late to be honoured and loved unconditionally!

13

Rite of passage
Recluse

The Lesson
Composting

The Age
Death

North

The colour of **Black**
The night, winter

THE EIGHTH AGE
Death

The zen definition of happiness:
First grandfather dies, then father dies, then son dies

THE RITE OF PASSAGE
RECLUSE
Separation - *He steps away from his family and community*
Transition - *He lets go*
Incorporation - *He becomes compost*

This book has been quite a journey for me, I have learnt a great deal in the researching of it, and remembered a great many things I had forgotten. We are now coming to the end of the book, and the end of the journey of life. I am scared of death; it frightens me, and yet I am also on occasions drawn towards it. There have been at least two moments in my life when I have been in situations where my life has been threatened. On both occasions it was only in retrospect that I realized my life was in danger. At the time I was too busy, too involved to really think about how dangerous the situation was. Too busy living to worry about dying – I hope that is the way it comes in the end. May we all pass gently and peacefully into the final stage.

181

To become a recluse is seen as a negative act in our society. Those who lock themselves away or choose to live a solitary life bring up issues around mental health and dysfunction. The recluse rite of passage is not so negative. To live as a recluse means not to be attached to anything, and not to take anything personally. The rite is a choice to be alone and move towards death. The individual needs to prepare for the next stage of being. In this time before his death, he needs to reflect. In order to reflect on his life he needs to be alone. This time is a very specific way of being. In the previous age he was able to reflect and share his experiences. This was a social reflection. He is now reflecting on his own, seeking his own company and not that of others. There is a great deal to be learnt from time alone, and each of us needs to be able to spend quality time by ourselves, not just when we are old.

Moksha

A man completes the cycle of life by dying, not becoming an elder. The act of dying is the mirror image of the act of conception. We come in, we go out. We have to be born to die, and we have to die in order to be born again. At least that's what I hope, but who knows? *'Look back at time... before our birth. In this way nature holds before our eyes the mirror of our future after death. Is this so grim, so gloomy?'*[15] When we have spent time alone with ourselves, we are able to see the real values of our actions, and to appreciate the futility or worth of most of it. We need to accept the inevitability of death, and in order to prepare for dying, we need to demystify death. All our lives move towards this point, and all our accumulation of knowledge and material goods mean nothing at this moment.

The grandfather is celebrated by his family and community, but he is moving away from them. He becomes very influential, makes decisions, imparts wisdom. He is active in politics and his views are sought by not just his family, but by the whole community. After a period of time, he becomes an elder, by initiating the teenagers. This completes his work so he can get up and leave. In the Hindu tradition he is called 'Sannyasa – the wandering recluse'. He gives away his home and his attachments and he becomes a hermit. By doing this he also completes the forgiveness process, as he lets go of all fears, hopes, duties and responsibilities. He looks towards 'Moksha – the release from the circle of birth and death'.

THE LESSON
Composting

When a seed first thrusts itself up from the soil, it is taking a huge risk, and it bravely persists with this ascent until it flowers. The moment it flowers it starts on an inevitable decline back to the soil where it will feed new seeds through its death. Our culture is fixated on being the flower; we don't see that there is an inevitability in the ascent and decline. The plant is never more beautiful at any one time; it is always beautiful, and it is always the same plant. When we become good, rich compost, we become a good ancestor – such should be the aspiration of us all.

I have a large compost area in my back garden, and it is the very heart of my endeavours. In it I pile all the vegetable waste from my kitchen, the grass cuttings, paper, cardboard and weeds – it takes the lot. It accepts the weeds as well as the flowers, and it changes them all, no judgements. Nettles, which are such an annoyance in the garden, become great composters. The amount of waste I put in can sometimes look immense and the pile becomes 6 foot tall or higher, and yet within weeks it's down and compacting, ready for more. In the heat that is generated live a multiplicity of worms, bugs and creatures. I love to see them working away. Earlier this month I pulled off the carpet covers, and there, curled up and happy, was a beautiful grass snake. It made me feel very happy. After two years of absorbing and fermenting, the pile is reduced to black rich soil, and I love to put my hands into it, to feel its damp potential. The compost pile feeds my vegetables; I put it onto the potatoes and seeds and they thrive. When we lose contact with the simple message of compost, we try to hold onto things. For me, this links into the idea that all those things we hold as precious and dear to us are inevitably not ours. We need to put everything into the compost pile, not just the weeds, but the precious flowers as well. If we are going to do this job well, we need to relinquish everything. As we become reclusive and begin to live simply and without frills, we realize the material goods and even the people in our lives are not 'ours'. They don't belong to us, just because we are related and we have lived together for many years. This is the real meaning of stepping away and becoming the recluse.

Bows and arrows

And a woman who held a babe against her bosom said, Speak to us of children. And he said:
Your children are not your children.
They are the sons and daughters of Life's longing for itself.
They come through you but not from you,
And though they are with you yet they belong not to you.
You may give them your love but not your thoughts,
For they have their own thoughts.
You may house their bodies but not their souls,
For their souls dwell in the house of [their] tomorrow, which you cannot visit, not even in your dreams.
You may strive to be like them, but seek not to make them like you.
For life goes not backward nor tarries with yesterday.
You are the bows from which your children as living arrows are sent forth.[*16]
I love that last line. It's saying, 'I am just the starting point from which my children will be propelled out into the world.' That doesn't diminish me, nor does it deny my love for my children, but it means I am able to see

184

the separate nature of myself and my loved ones, and this allows me to step towards death with a little less fear.

THE AGE
Death
We are now in the end game of life in the physical realm. Death is near and it can become a key focus. How we deal with death will often reflect the way in which we have lived. If we have been active, hopeful and loving, then we often pass in that way. If we have been fearful and worried, then we often pass that way too. My great-uncle, Van, was a great role model. He passed away in his sleep sat peacefully in the corner of the departure lounge in Heathrow airport, with a rucksack on his back and a smile on his face. Way to go.

Simplification
If we can simplify our lives right down, then we reduce our desires and our needs. By doing this correctly we reach a state of being where death is just a small step rather than a huge leap. By composting and letting go we reach a place where we no longer take things personally, where we are no longer a stakeholder in the meaning and importance of being. We will live on in those who knew us. In life and in death we are remembered by our families and by our community. We live on in our children and those we have influenced. If we stop taking it all so seriously, we can see that our input into the world will continue long after we are gone. To believe in this we need to have an understanding of and sympathy for spirituality.

Spirituality
Spirituality is a pretty contentious word, and I can only explain how I relate to it. Science is our religion nowadays, and many people believe absolutely in our ability to either prove or disprove everything. I don't

agree with these people. Those who pursue religious beliefs have mostly constructed a similar paradigm, only instead of a man in a white coat, they have a man with a white beard making all the decisions and proving the case. Mostly this man is a judgmental type who never forgets your wrongs. I don't agree with these people either. While I value what human beings have achieved on this earth, I don't hold with them as the supreme pinnacle of evolution. I know there are much larger, more comprehensive forces at work out there, and this belief allows me to have faith in the innate good within us, and our ability to connect to a number of greater forces or energies that can help us and enable us to stay within the positive. I believe in a holistic spirituality, a non-judgemental or religious sense of there being more to life than just life itself.

Progression from life to death

By believing we are sophisticated, modern and Godless, we have created a society that does not serve or nurture our souls or spirituality. As babies, we are left to cry in our cots; as children, our wonder is suppressed; as teenagers, we are outlawed and expected to peer-initiate ourselves; as fathers, we are stressed and confused; as grandfathers, we become disillusioned and miserable; as elders, we are ghettoized and ignored; our deaths pass un-mourned and with suppressed grief. I want my generation to step up and away from such a scenario. The development of these ages of men is vitally important in the creation of a new way of being for the following generations. Without an understanding of the importance of generations, the roles they have to play and the ways in which rites of passage can assist us, we are contemplating a very bleak and miserable future.

Death is always the final act of any society or life. We live in such a suppressed, fearful and guilt-ridden culture that we have tried to eliminate death, and our relationship to it has become distorted and

186

unnatural. We have sanitized and artificially lit our world and environment, and by doing so we have lost contact with shadow and death. Absorbed in our fear and shame, we have lost all contact with how to be around them. They come as strangers; we are surprised and fearful in their presence. Inevitably, by trying to ignore and cheat death, we bring it closer to us – such is the paradox of existence. We are the generation who really can extinguish all human life on the planet. What a remarkable development that is – uniquely our generation faces this dilemma. We have created this possibility, and we live now on the precious edge of extinction. Our generation is the one needing to face up to death, and we feel wholly unprepared and inadequate. It is not too late. We can still grow to appreciate death and the wonder of composting. In order to do this well, we need to live positive lives full of wonder and joy and remain in the flow as much as possible. We need to take risks, be challenged, make mistakes, try again, be frustrated, fall in love, live in passion, do the things we were born to do. When we lead such lives we can come to the end of them without regrets and without resentment. If we have truly lived through the ages, we can come to a place of forgiveness and acceptance.

Grandfather Stone
I come from the magma at the core of the Earth, at the centre of the Mother.
I flow up through the ground
That's how I start out
As pure energy, life force
I flow out of the One Heart and consume everything in my path.
You can do this
You have to risk everything
In order to make the magma flow
If you don't, it won't flow
If you hold back it will not manifest.
When the magma is flowing and coming out of you

You don't make it solid
It's the air, the weather, the other elements which solidify the magma
It's how other people hear you that solidifies your wisdom.
Don't personalise your wisdom
Just flow and let others solidify it for you
Layer upon layer
There is no end to this process.
If you do it right, in the right spirit, with heart
The magma is solidified in such a way that it becomes diamonds
That sparkle and are pure, solid and really hard
The eyes of our children's children

This is the last of the teachings I received through my shamanic journeying with elders. Grandfather Stone is telling us how to live. Be a conduit, enable life to flow through and out of yourself. By being in the flow, the layers you create will become solid; they will have meaning and resonance. When you die, you will be remembered; you will be present still, and you'll sparkle in the eyes of your children. You cannot ask for more.

THE PAST

Almost all our ancestors, almost all the indigenous people of the planet, believed in reincarnation. Of all the human beings to have lived on the planet, only a very small percentage have not believed in reincarnation, in life after death in its many different forms. We have created a post-modern culture that is sophisticated, urban, scientific and sanitized. In this culture we have not only excluded death and shadow, but we have also excluded the possibility of life after death as well. Science cannot prove or disprove reincarnation. It is up to the individual to come to his/her own conclusions, and I would never seek to force my views on others. If we don't believe in reincarnation, then we can be fearful about death. If we believe in reincarnation, we can still be fearful, but there is a sense of hope, some light at the end of the tunnel, not perpetual darkness! However we come at it, death is inevitable. A society that is open and accepting of death is more holistic and realistic. A truly sophisticated society accepts death.

The day of the dead

To become sophisticated we need to create respect and an honouring of death, and the Mexican tradition is a bright example of a residue from rituals and beliefs which used to be held all over the world. The Day of the Dead (El Día de los Muertos or All Souls' Day) is around the 2nd of November. On this day, family and friends pray for and remember friends and family members who have died. To do so, they build private altars honouring the deceased, using sugar skulls, marigolds, the favourite foods and beverages of the departed, and visit the graves with these as gifts. Similar holidays are celebrated in many parts of the world the Dia de Finados in Brazil, where many Brazilians celebrate by visiting cemeteries and churches. In Spain, there are festivals and parades, and at the end of the day, people gather at cemeteries and pray for their loved ones who have died. Similar observances occur elsewhere in Europe and in the Philippines, and similarly-themed celebrations appear in many Asian and African cultures. They enable people to take time out and to grieve properly and fully, not choke it back and suppress it.

Bahá'í religion

'The world beyond is as different from this world as this world is different from that of the child while still in the womb of its mother.' The analogy to the womb in many ways summarizes the Bahá'í view of earthly existence. Just as the womb constitutes an important place for a person's initial physical development, the physical world provides the matrix for the development of the individual soul. Bahá'ís view life as a sort of workshop, where one can develop and perfect those qualities needed in the next life.

189

Qur'an 3:133
Again looking at individual forgiveness and the expectation of rewards in the afterlife for those who have been righteous, the Qur'an advises: *'Be quick in the race for forgiveness from your Lord, and for a Garden whose width is that (of the whole) of the heavens and of the earth, prepared for the righteous.'*

We can become embroiled in unhelpful religious or scientific diatribes about the afterlife. If we live life to the full and try to do good by others, then we may be moving towards enlightenment and peace on our own. I don't think any of us would say that to live our lives with such aspirations is a waste of time. Whether there is a life after death becomes irrelevant when we are in the flow of being authentic and living a fulfilling life.

THE PRESENT

In our society we have turned away from death. We would rather not look if at all possible. *'Getting old isn't easy for a lot of us. Neither is living, neither is dying. We struggle against the inevitable and we all suffer because of it.'*[17] We have lost connection to the idea of our inevitable composting, of the shadow, the earth and the dirt. This manifests in how we seek to sanitize our lives, and how we suppress grief.

Sanitizing our lives

We have given over the responsibility for our health and wellbeing to science, and the mantra of the scientist is 'cleanse and purify for better or for worse'. When this combines with the interest of big business and the bottom line of profit margins, then all sorts of justifications and mysteries are concocted to support 'sanitation'. The pasteurization of milk takes all bad enzymes out, and destroys everything good in it as well. It literally neutralizes milk. There are many other products we happily and ignorantly consume whose histories are tales of irresponsibility and the drive for profit and sanitation over common sense. We have created huge industries to ensure we are not contaminated by, on the whole, very helpful bugs and germs. We are seeking solace in cleanliness and the suppression of emotions. Dirt is good; we live on the Earth; we are nourished by the soil.

The suppression of grief
In our pasteurized bubble of safety, we believe that to express, and to participate in, grief is to be vulnerable and weak. Grief is a magnificent emotional response to loss. In its raw form, like milk, it is complete and enriching; in its suppressed and weakened form, it is thin and can be harmful. Grief comes from loss and is most commonly associated with bereavement. It is a natural state of being, and is with us at certain key points in our lives. If we are able to express our grief and to fully come to terms with the loss, we are able to move on and form new connections. If the grief is suppressed and inhibited, we will often fall ill, be unable to move on and suffer with psychological and physical ailments. Men, as a generalization, suffer most from the suppression of grief. The past generations of men were taught from an early age that they shouldn't cry, that they needed to be strong and should have a stiff upper lip. By being given these messages our fathers and grandfathers suppressed and withheld their emotions for years and years. Not surprisingly this can lead to deep psychological problems, and inappropriate responses to seemingly minor hurts or slights. The next generations need to be liberated from such oppressive views, and we are definitely changing. We are moving towards more emotionally intelligent men and a healthier relationship with loss and death.

The cultural experience of the Mexican people around the time of the Day of the Dead is a huge emotional clearing of the suppressed and repressed feelings of the previous twelve months. In recent times the sweeping response by the British public to the death of Princess Diana came as a surprise. It was just a physical manifestation of a mass emotional response. Many used it as a time to clear stress and emotions built up over the years. Grief, when expressed wholly and completely, is not just a personal experience; it can also be a mass experience. The poet Robert Bly talks about America, and particularly American men, as having not grieved properly for many years. He says the lack of correct grief for the wars in Korea and Vietnam, let alone the more recent ones, has created an emotionally stunted generation of men. I agree, and we can only ask that the next generations are given the time and chance to express their grief fully and without judgment.

THE FUTURE

Surely, if we are emotionally intelligent and able to grieve, we will step towards our own death with a far more enlightened tread. If we include death in our lives, then it won't come as such a huge shock and be so frightening. There are so many ways we can do this. Here are just some examples:

Princess Diana

Something new happened in 1997 when Princess Diana died. The whole of Britain was joined in the expression of grief for her passing. It took people by surprise, but it marked a positive move. May we have more such occasions!

Roadside memorials

In recent years in Britain there is a roadside phenomenon that has grown inordinately and without remark. Our roads are now adorned with memorials, altars, flowers and wreaths, marking the place of fatal accidents. Twenty years ago such memorials were not present, and yet now they are a common feature of our roads and motorways. Somehow it has become popular to mark these places, and I'm all in favour of it.

Bright cemeteries

Linked to this is the increased floral and decorative adornment of our cemeteries. The inclusion of seats, children's play areas, gardens and many other features for the living increases the number of people visiting such places. Our austere, bleak and stony Victorian cemeteries are being adorned, brightened and enlivened. I'm all in favour of this too!

Diverse funerals

Funerals don't have to be the boring and religious experiences of the past. We can have inter-faith celebrations; we can decorate and have ecologically sound caskets. We can sing songs and dance to any number of tunes. We can smile and cry at the memory of a passed friend, and we don't have to wear black. I'm very much in favour of all these things. They all lead to a great understanding of, and ease with, death.

We need to be familiar with death throughout our lives

Whilst we are working out in the woods with the street-wise teenagers who think they are hard and tough, we often bring in a man who is an expert at trapping rabbits. He traps and kills sufficient rabbits for our supper, and the teenagers are shown the results and told that we have to skin and cook the rabbits. Many turn vegetarian instantly on the spot. They have never been confronted by the dead animal prior to it being de-boned and hermetically sealed in plastic. We cannot afford to allow our children to avoid such responsibility. Seeing the consequences of their desires and needs opens their minds. We seem to think that our present way of being (where everything is pre-packed and sanitized) is natural, but it is wholly unnatural, and within living memory things were very different. My grandfather told me of his experience in a small farming community when a family slaughtered their pig. It was a great celebration and the whole community was summoned to witness the event. The pig was tethered by its back legs and hung, alive, in a large room. Everyone gathered, and the pig's throat was cut. Those splashed by the blood were being blessed and being reminded of the shared responsibilities of the community.

We can then come to a place of acceptance and understanding

My great aunt knew she was very ill and the doctors wanted her to go to hospital and be cared for there. She knew what she wanted. She summoned her close family to her, said her goodbyes and then told her children that she wanted to die. They stayed with her, but she didn't eat or drink, and then she died in her bed, surrounded by her family. I am not as strong-willed as my great aunt, but the example she set has certainly made me think. Will I really want to have my life extended through drugs, hospitalization and care when I really have so little to live for? Having developed Parkinson's disease, my father was in hospital and in a very poor state of health towards the end of his life; however, he continued to talk of returning home and being in his bed. When the hospital moved him into a care home and he realized he was never going to return to his home and his bed he died the next day.

We are in control

At present, we live in fear of our own untimely death – the car crash, suicide or murder. All seem to have a high risk of occurring and the news is full of such incidents. In reality, however, these represent only a small minority of deaths. Accidents account for 4% of all deaths in America, suicide 1%, and murder less than 1%. The great majority of us will die of natural causes, or diseases brought on by our lifestyle (heart disease and cancer). In order to go quietly and well into that dark night, we need to remember how it all started – with conception. At the beginning of the baby's existence, the womb must feel like a huge and cavernous dwelling. The baby in the womb only ever lives in water, has never breathed air and has all his needs catered for by his mother. The womb represents his whole world. Just before he is born this perfect dwelling place restricts him; he has grown so huge that he can no longer stay within its confines. He must move out, because he has outgrown his world. As a consequence of the move from the one world to the next he can experience pain, remorse, guilt and any number of emotions, but most importantly, it is a non-reversible move – there is no going back. Once through the birthing canal he struggles for breath. He is surrounded by a completely foreign substance – air – which he has never breathed before, and he has to learn very quickly how to breathe. He enters the next huge world. He moves towards the light. In those early moments his new surroundings are completely alien, incomprehensible and beyond his experience and previous understanding in terms of their size, dimension and viability to sustain his life.

Welcome to the next world little wise one!

SUGGESTIONS FOR ACTION
Good death
I'll die when I'm good and ready, and I'm ready now. I have achieved a great deal in my short time on earth. I am so lucky to be the father of my two children, to have been in loving and nurturing relationships and to have been employed all over the world to do the work I enjoy. A friend remarked the other day, 'you are paid to talk about being you; it doesn't get much better than that'. No it doesn't. I am blessed, and I still have a great many things I want to do and see. If I am to be knocked down by a bus tomorrow, then so be it. There is no need for regret whilst alive. I wish that we could all move to this place with compassion and understanding, not fear.

Funerals
I have a friend, John Fox, who has been a mentor and teacher for many years. He wrote a book many years ago called *The Dead Good Funeral Guide,* from which I quote the recommendations for improvement:
• *When someone dies at home, keeping the body in the house may*

195

be positive and comforting for some families, depending on the circumstances of the death and on the house or flat, but harder for a single person left to cope unsupported. The opportunity to spend some time over the leave-taking on familiar territory, to exclude strangers from handling the body and to decide what clothes will be worn in the coffin can all contribute to making the funeral personal. There are very few technical problems with keeping a body in the house for three days or so, as long as a cool room can be provided. Help with laying out can be provided by a district nurse. What is needed is a change in the present attitude from funeral directors who automatically whisk the body away, for everyone's comfort and collect the usual fees. This implies forfeiting several usual fees. Many people will want this service, but the choice, the possibility, should be there, and as ever, it is better if the preference has been thought about in advance.

•   Scheduling was the issue that people felt most strongly about. Mourners should have as much time in the crematorium as they need. There should be no overlap, no queues. In an ideal situation no funeral should see another funeral. Funeral directors may well throw their hands up in horror, but it is important to ask in whose favour are the schedules drawn up. If you particularly want a funeral early in the morning, or in the evening at sunset, or at a weekend, why should it not be possible? The current regimentation comes from an outmoded attitude toward providing a service. We currently get buried or cremated Monday to Friday 9 - 5, or more like 10 - 4. It uncannily parallels the extraordinary number of babies born in hospital within the same shifts.

•   Flexibility in layout could be offered not so much in chapels but in crematoria, since many modern ones do not have fixed seating. It could be re-arranged from the formal rows all facing each other, to a semicircle or horseshoe, or a circle even where mourners can make eye contact with each other. It could be removed altogether, to accommodate cultural and religious diversity such as kneeling on the carpet to pray, or sitting in a circle on the floor, or wilder options altogether - like dancing! Temporary decorations, bringing in personal objects for the service, should be permitted. With co-operation and goodwill this could work, because it is always going to be a minority choice. People asking for a longer time could reasonably be offered

196

the last appointment of the day, to facilitate preparation before and putting things straight afterwards.
•   Support for the DIY funeral service and the needs of the arrangers should be offered. This may include turning off the recorded music and removing the religious artefacts visible in the church. 'At the end we said no music specifically and they played piped music.'
•   Regulations about memorials could be relaxed, to permit a wider choice of materials, less control of design, more freedom to make a hand-crafted (non-standard) memorial in wood or stone carving, or maybe a durable mosaic. These objects have a place, made as an act of love and made to a high standard. Why should machined slabs of alien granite in marble with computer generated lettering constitute the aesthetic that is held up for everyone to conform to? The use of natural pieces of local stone will offer a habitat for lichen and mosses, which bring their own beauty. It might also help to keep a small quarry going, in preference to the exploitative trade of importing shiploads of marble at rip-off prices from third world countries - the source that most monumental masons use. Hand-carved lettering may not be immaculate, but it retains the human touch.

Practical thoughts from someone who has given time and effort to the matter.

Eulogies
The start of the changes in our relationship to death and funerals are there to be seen. Let's build on them in the next years. Some people are now having their eulogies and services before they die, and I like this idea. When my father died, my mother asked me to write something. I spent about a week working on it, and by doing so I came to a place of deep understanding and compassion for my father. The speech I gave was full of love and appreciation for him and his life. I would have preferred to say those words to him whilst he was alive, but his passing gave me the opportunity for reflection, and to honour him.

Death is the giver of such opportunities, thank you.

CONCLUSIONS
The Journey

From conception to death

A man is conceived in an act of love, during a mutual exchange full of respect, passion and consciousness. He brings this awareness and significance of physical being into the universe.

He goes through the rite of passage which is conception.
In the womb he is nurtured and fed by his mother and father. He receives lessons from his ancient ancestors, the fish, the bird, and he is introduced to abundance. He brings the awareness and importance of abundance into his life.

He goes through birth.
As a baby he is held, praised and welcomed. His placenta is honoured and respected. He is shown how to give to others, how by giving of himself he will enable them to grow. He brings the awareness and importance of giving and receiving into his life.

He goes through the rite of first footing.
He connects completely with the earth, he runs and walks. He is encouraged and supported in his exploration of the world. He expresses himself in wonder and awe. He makes mistakes, he encounters pain. He brings the awareness and importance of exploration and wonder into his life.

He goes through the rite of bravery.
He is able to leave his parents' house. He finds his peers and comrades. He is encouraged and recognized by elders. He seeks to find his soul's purpose. He explores his sensuality and sexuality. He brings the awareness and importance of questioning into his life.

He becomes a father.
He understands how to be responsible, to nurture and support. He joins with another and creates a third. He pursues his soul's purpose. He brings the awareness and importance of responsibility into his life.

He becomes a grandfather.
He starts to give away his accumulations, he teaches others and is recognized by his wider community. He brings the awareness and importance of giving away into his life.

He goes through the rite of becoming an elder.
He supports teenagers. He forgives himself and those around him. He continues to give away. He brings the awareness and importance of forgiveness into his life.

He reflects before death.
He is able to come to terms with who he is, he sees he has fulfilled his soul's purpose and he knows he has done as well as he could. He brings the awareness and importance of composting into his life.

A time of crisis

We are all acutely aware that there are faults and failings within the current liberal capitalist culture we have created. Our very existence on the planet is now at a tipping point, and we have reached a precarious place. Whichever way we look – to the numbers of starving and ill people, the detrimental environmental damage of the planet, the inadequacies of our banks, governments and leaders – there is a crisis. A time of crisis calls for revolutionary changes. Many of us have chosen not to look. We have remained unaffected, and continue to perpetuate a belief system based on fear and shame. As human beings, we have perpetuated myths, we have created illusions and we are now being confronted with some painful truths.

Uninitiated men

One of those truths is that we have uninitiated men and directionless, rudderless boys, who are seeking guidance but don't know where to turn. Our boys are failing academically, they are violent, believe being tough is the answer and they are miserable, discontented and unfulfilled. This state of mind and being is fed by any number of other factors – lack of role models, wars, greed, famine, materialistic attitudes and selfish concepts that toughen and create peer pressure. To deal with boys and men in isolation is impossible. We all need to become awake; we all need to embrace change. This book offers some of my thoughts and ideas on the masculine aspect of the overall crisis. Please take it as a starting point, as a tiny drop in the vast ocean. Without such tiny drops the ocean will not come into existence.

Being recognized

For me, the idea that men undergo changes in their lives as they mature is fundamental to my understanding of life. At present we seem to expect our boys to become men without help, guidance or recognition. We bemoan the lack of respect and community in our society, and yet we do nothing to create it. By honouring (recognizing) that boys have become men and that grandfathers have become elders, we create the opportunities to celebrate community and respect. Rites of passage are essential tools in this journey. By enabling older men to help younger men we create a bond perpetuating community and respect. Since the industrial revolution we deliberately moved away from these ideas and concepts, and the damaging consequences of such a move are all around us. This book outlines the concept of 8 ages, and attached to those ages the essences or lessons needing to be learnt. I hope we can learn them. I am promoting the ideal of rites being supervised by elders, but recognizing this is not always possible, this work just needs to be done in whatever way possible.

Men are not ignorant, violent and immature. Men can be positive. All of us, men and women alike, have the same natures – the capacity to be loving, caring and generous. It is the way in which we nurture our men which is the failing. I believe that if we give men the right conditions to grow and mature in, they will become emotionally intelligent, capable of distinguishing between violence and aggression. If men were assisted in their maturation by undertaking a series of rites, then the focus on self, war, hate, fear and materialism would diminish. I know a lot of men have not been able to do this vital work, and I am facilitating the opportunity for men to undertake such rites retrospectively. The men who come on these workshops and rites all agree they are necessary, and the rites have led to positive changes in their circumstances. This is just the start of something. I'm not suggesting we all return to the Stone Age, that our ancestors or indigenous people had it right and we are completely wrong. I'm saying we need to open out the way in which we travel from being a youth to maturity, and an examination of our past can lead to a more holistic approach to the future. We all need to be involved in this debate, men and women both, and I would hope it will allow us all to gain a better understanding of ourselves and others, without so much judgment and prejudice.

Spiritually advanced

In recent years I have come across many women (and quite a large number of men) who believe that women are better than men. The idea that women are more spiritually advanced and sorted, while men remain basically rapists, aggressors or children. I have to disagree. Just as it would be offensive to say that white people are more advanced than black people, we cannot make such assumptions, judgments and wildly inaccurate statements. They only perpetuate inferiority and guilt. A while

202

ago Grandfather Wallace Black Elk came to Wales, blessed be his memory, and whilst he was here we performed rituals and ceremonies with him. One day as an aside he said to me, 'It's good to be amongst white people like you.' When I asked why, he replied, 'Normally the white people I come across in America are full of guilt and shame. You lot aren't, you're more like red people.' No one person or race is more spiritual, more advanced, or more complete than anyone else. We are all at the same evolutionary stage, and we are all one species. Some people seem to be more content, seem to be happier than others. In the end, we have the same capacity for joy and love within us as the next man or woman; we only see in others that which we already have.

Fear and guilt

In our materialist society we are ruled by fear and guilt. The fear of loss is everything, and it motivates us to continue our exponential journey towards the destruction of our planet. Some of the fear arises because we don't receive recognition. If I recognize myself as a good father, then I will remember the good times when I was active, and not beat myself up over other times. By doing so, I actually encourage myself to become a good father. How we do the recognition work is down to us as individuals. Rites of passage can be used to recognize who we are and who we have become. The great majority of men on the planet have not recognized their own potential, and many old men still behave like teenagers and children. If we can encourage men to come to terms with their own development and evolution, and to be satisfied with their progress, rather than wanting to be somewhere else, we will affect a huge amount of change on the planet. Just by becoming who we are right now, we will lose a huge amount of shame and guilt, and we will be able to move forward with less fear. That is what I seek for myself, and this is my radical and revolutionary message: 'accept yourself as you are right now.' By doing so you will bring about positive change in the world.

It has been a moving and enlightening journey for me to write this book. I have enjoyed and struggled with it, probably in equal measure. This book was started during the last year of writing the previous one, *Using The Ugly Duckling to find the Missing Link between Boys and Men*. As I have completed this one, I am already making notes toward the next. The distillation and giving away process is on-going. Thank you for coming with me. Blessings on your journey. Be kind to yourself, for you are doing the best you can. Until we meet again.

Quotes and references

Chapter Two
"Muratare – Circumcision" Film available from:
www.soundoftheheart.com

Chapter Three
"Zorba the Buddha" Film available from:
www.iosho.com/TheLifeofOsho/08-04-personal.htm
"The Duluth Domestic Abuse Intervention Project"
www.theduluthmodel.org/15-04-2010

Chapter Four
*1 S. Keen, *Fire in the belly: on being a man*, Bantam, New York, 1991.

Chapter Five
"The Seven Ages Of Men" Film available from:
www.soundoftheheart.com
Rites of passage, based on:
A. v. Gennep, *Rites of passage: a classic study of cultural celebrations,* University of Chicago, Chicago, 1960.

Chapter Six
*2 G. Saint-Pierre and D. Shapiro, *The metamorphic technique: principles and practice*, Element, London, 1982.

Chapter Seven
*3 C. Royer, and others, *Discussion sur la couvades,* Bulletins de la Societe d'Anthropologie de Paris, 3rd series, Paris 1882.

Chapter Eight
Working with fathers, workshops and courses available from:
www.fatherskills.co.uk

Chapter Nine

Teenage rites of passage, more information in book
"Using The Ugly Duckling to find the Missing Link between Boys and Men"
available from: www.soundoftheheart.com
Film *"Kevin and Perry Go Large"* 2000
*4 W. Cannon, *Bodily changes in pain, hunger, fear and rage*, Appleton, New York 1915.
Flight or fight, based on:
C. Darwin, *On the origin of species,* John Murray, London, 1859.
Teenagers and porn, more information:
www.menagainstporn.org
*5 S. Biddulph, *Manhood: an action plan for changing men's lives,* Hawthorn, Stroud, 1994.
"Muratare – Circumcision" Film available from:
www.soundoftheheart.com
*6 L. Peltier, *Prison writings- my life is my sundance,* St. Matin's Press, New York, 1999.
*7 M. Karlin, *Coming of age on the street: ritual invention and the sacred in American gang initiation rituals,* Mythic Imagination Institute 2008.

Chapter Ten

*8 D. J. Tracey, *Remaking men: Jung, spirituality and social change,* Routledge, London 1997.
*9 R. Bly, *Iron john: a book about men,* Element: Dorset 1990.
*10 and 11 N. Hall, and W. R. Dawson, *Broodmales,* Spring, Dallas, 1989.
*12 J. Embling, *Fragmented lives: a darker side of Australian life,* Penguin, Melbourne, 1986.
*13 H. Goldberg, *The new male: from macho to sensitive but still all male,* Signet, New York, 1980.
Working with fathers, workshops and courses available from:
www.fatherskills.co.uk

Chapter Eleven
Indigenous Peoples and Sustainable Development at the:
International Institute for Sustainable Development, Winnipeg, 1992
www.Bhagavad-Gita.org

Chapter Twelve
Outdoor learning and environmental education specialists, more information:
www.circleofliferediscovery.com
*14 G. Saint-Pierre and D. Shapiro, *The metamorphic technique: principles and practice*, Element, London, 1982.
More information on the Elders available at:
www.theelders.org

Chapter Thirteen
*15 Lucretius, *On the nature of the universe*, Latham, reg. trans., Penguin Classics, London, 1951.
*16 K. Gibran, *The prophet*, Heinemann, London, 1926.
*17 R. Dass, *Still here*, Penguin Putnam, New York, 2000.
"The Dead Good Funerals Book" available from:
www.welfare-state.org

Where other quotations have been used, every reasonable effort has been made to seek permission and include full accreditation of the source prior to publication.

Selected bibliography

A. Adler, *Understanding human nature*, George Allen & Unwin, London, 1928.

S. Baron-Cohen, *The essential difference: men, women & the extreme male brain*, Penguin, London 2004.

J. Baumgardner, and A. Richards, *Manifesta: young women, feminism, and the future*, Farrar, Straus and Giroux, New York, 2000.

S. Biddulph, *Manhood: an action plan for changing men's lives*, Hawthorn, Stroud, 1994.

D. Blankenhorn, *Fatherless America: confronting our most urgent social problem*, Basic, New York, 1995.

R. Bly, *Iron john: a book about men*, Element: Dorset 1990.

J. A. Burrow, *The ages of man: A study in medieval writing and thought*, Oxford, London, 1986.

J. Campbell, *The hero with a thousand faces*, Princetown University, Princetown, 1970.

W. Cannon, *Bodily changes in pain, hunger, fear and rage*, Appleton, New York 1915.

R. Carson, *Silent spring*, Houghton Mifflin, Boston, 1962.

A. Clare, *On men: masculinity in crisis*, Chatto & Windus, London, 2000.

H. Clements, *Alfred russel wallace*, Hutchinson and Co, London, 1983.

G. Dalbey, *Healing the masculine soul,* Word, Melbourne, 1989.

T. Dalrymple, *Our culture: what's left of it,* Ivan R. Dee, Chicago, 2005

R. B. Dancy, *You are your child's first teacher,* Celestial, Berkeley, California, 1989.

C. Darwin, *On the origin of species,* John Murray, London, 1859.

R. Dass, *Still here,* Penguin Putnam, New York, 2000.

J. Diamond, *The rise and fall of the third chimpanzee*, Radius, London, 1991.

J. Donne, *Devotions upon emergent occasions and several steps in my sickness,* Meditation XVII, 1624.

M. Eliade, *Rites and symbols of initiation: the mysteries of birth and rebirth,* Harper, London, 1958.

D. and J. Elium, *Raising a son: parenting and the making of a healthy man,* Hawthorn, Stroud, 1992.

J. Embling, *Fragmented lives: a darker side of Australian life,* Penguin, Melbourne, 1986.

E. H. Erikson, *Childhood and Society,* 2nd ed., Norton, New York, 1963.
      Identity and the life cycle, Norton, New York, 1980.

A. v. Gennep, *Rites of passage: a classic study of cultural celebrations,* University of Chicago, Chicago, 1960.

K. Gibran, *The prophet,* Heinemann, London, 1926.

E. J. Gold, *The American book of the dead,* Gateway, Nevada, CA, 1975.

H. Goldberg, *The new male: from macho to sensitive but still all male,* Signet, New York, 1980.

J. Gray, *Men are from mars, women are from venus,* Thorsons, London, 1993.

M. Gurian, *What could he be thinking? A guide to the mysteries of a man's mind,* Element, London, 2004.

N. Hall, and W. R. Dawson, *Broodmales,* Spring, Dallas, 1989.

M. Hardiman, *Ordinary heroes: a future for men,* New Leaf, Dublin, 2000.

J. Hillman, *A blue fire,* Harper Collins, London, 1989.

J. Hollis, *The middle passage: from misery to meaning in midlife,* University of Toronto: Canada, 1993.

R. Horrocks, *Masculinity in crisis,* St Martin's Press, New York, 1994.

T. Ivens and N. Clements, *An introduction to working with fathers,* Fatherskills, Wales, 2005.

R. Jensen, *Getting off: pornography and the end of masculinity,* South End Press, Cambridge, Mass., 2007.

C. G. Jung, *Psyche and symbol,* Doubleday, New York, 1958.

S. Keen, *Fire in the belly: on being a man,* Bantam, New York, 1991.

T. Klein, *Celebrating life:rites of passage for all ages,* Delphi, London, 1992.

P. Kropotkin, *Mutual aid: a factor of evolution*, William Heinemann, London, 1902.

Modern science and anarchism, Freedom, London, 1912.

J. Lee, *At my father's wedding*, Bantam, New York, 1991.

D. J. Levinson, *The seasons of a man's life*, Ballantine, New York, 1977.

J. Liedloff, *The continuum concept*, Penguin, London, 1989.

K. Lorenz, *The waning of humaneness*, Unwin, London, 1988.

Lucretius, *On the nature of the universe*, Latham, reg. trans., Penguin Classics, London, 1951.

H. C. Macnamara, *Media and male identity: the making and remaking of men*, Palgrave Macmillan, New York, 2006.

M. Meade, *Men and the water of life: initiation and the tempering of men*, Harper, London, 1993.

K. Meadows, *The medicine way*, Element, Dorset, 1990.

V. Megre, *Anastasia*, Ringing Cedars Press, Carmel, 1996.

A. d. Mello, *Awareness*, Fount, London, 1990.

M. Miedzian, *Boys will be boys*, Virago, London, 1992.

A. Miller, *For your own good*, Farar, Straus and Giroux, New York, 1983.

S. Miller, *Men and friendship*, Gateway, London, 1983.

A. Mitscherlich, *Society without the father*, Tavistock, London, 1969.

A. and B. Moir, *Why men don't iron: the new reality of gender differences*, Harper Collins, London, 1999.

L. Neall, *About our boys: a practical guide to bringing out the best in boys*, Neall Scott, Leighton Buzzard, 2007.

A. S. Neil, *Summerhill school: a new view of childhood*, Penguin, London, 1992.

R.Parke, & A.Brott,*Throwaway dads: the myths and barriers that keep men from being the fathers they want to be*, Houghton Mifflin, Boston, 1999.

K. Parker, *Save the males: why men matter why women should care*, Random, New York, 2008

L. Peltier, *Prison writings, my life is my sundance*, St. Matin's Press, New York, 1999.

M. Prechtel, *Secrets of the talking jaguar*, Element, London, 1998.

W. Pudney, and J. Cottrell, *Beginning fatherhood: a guide for expectant fathers*, Finch, Australia, 1998.

G. Saint-Pierre and D. Shapiro, *The metamorphic technique: principles and practice*, Element, London, 1982.

E. Sears, *The ages of man: medieval interpretations of the life cycle*, Princetown, New Jersey, 1986.

G. Sheehy, *Understanding men's passages: discovering the new map of men's lives*, Ballantine, New York, 1999

M. Some, *Of water and the spirit: ritual, magic and initiation in the life of an African shaman*, Tarcher/Putnam, London, 1994.

Ritual, power, healing and community, Gateway, Bath, 2000.

L. Sax, *Why gender matters: what parents and teachers need to know about the emerging science of sex difference*, Doubleday, New York, 2005.

C. Spezzano, *If it hurts, it isn't love: secrets of successful relationships*, Hodder and Stoughton, London 1991.

H. Storm, *Seven arrows*, Harper and Row, New York, 1972.

K. Thompson (Editor), *To be a man: in search of the deep masculine*, Jeremy Tarcher, Los Angeles, 1991.

L. Tiger, *The decline of the males*, St. Martins Press, New York, 1999.

B. Torbert and Associates, *Action inquiry: the secret of timely and transforming leadership*, Berrett-Koehler Publishers, San Fransisco. 2000.

D. J. Tracey, *Remaking men*, Routledge, London 1997.

J. D. Vigil, *Group Processes and Street Identity: Adolescent Chicano Gang Members*, Ethos 16, no. 4: 421-45. 1998.

A. R. Wallace, *Studies scientific and social*, Macmillan, London, 1900.

B. Weiner, *Boy into man: a fathers' guide to initiation of teenage sons*, Transformation, London, 1992.

P. A. Weiss, *Hierarchically organized systems in theory and practice*, Hafner, New York, 1971.

Resources

Nick Clements

Books

Creative Collaboration
A radical and extraordinary book which challenges the present art dogmas and beliefs. It offers new and innovative approaches to create remarkable new ways of living, collaborating and developing society. It offers inspiration and guidance to those who want to create such opportunities in the future.
ISBN: 978-0-9547302-1-5

Using the Ugly Duckling to find The Missing Link between boys and men
Using the concept of rites of passage with a recent translation of *"The Ugly Duckling"* Nick Clements shows how they can be used to deal with issues around teenagers. This is a provocative book about parenting boys and how to develop constructive relationships with them. Well worth reading as a parent.
ISBN: 978-0-9547302-2-2
Both books are available from www.soundoftheheart.com

Workshops and projects

www. soundoftheheart.com
Sound of the heart publications
The website for details of the work of Nick Clements and associates. Information on books, workshops and films.
www.fatherskills.co.uk
Fatherskills
Information on training courses for professionals working with fathers. Pioneers in the development of training for professionals working with

men. Promoting family life, increasing fathers participation, empowering families to reach their full potential. Working alongside local authorities to create and develop inclusive strategies for men and fathers.
www.circleofliferediscovery.co.uk
Circle of Life Rediscovery
Information on a Community Interest Company that runs eco-sessions, woodland days, programmes, camps and youth trainings for young people.
www.valleyandvale.co.uk
Valley and Vale Community Arts
Offering access to Community Arts and media workshops and projects in video, animation, dance, drama, forum theatre, photography, visual and digital arts, multi media, music and design creating equal opportunities through positive action by prioritising individuals, groups and communities who are often marginalized.
www.heavenandbirth.com
Heaven and Birth
Provide holistic birth preparation which combines ancient wisdom, self-discovery and simple ritual with modern midwifery care.

Parenting in the UK
www.c4eo.org.uk
The Centre for Excellence and Outcomes in Children and Young People's Services
Aims to share and promote good practice in the delivery of Every Child Matters outcomes.
www.childreninscotland.org.uk
Children in Scotland
Is a national agency for voluntary, statutory and professional organisations working with children and their families in Scotland.

www.childreninwales.org.uk
Children in Wales
Is the national umbrella children's organisation in Wales to meet the needs of children, young people and their families.

www.familyandparenting.org
The Family and Parenting Institute
Role is to bring together organisations, knowledge and know-how to enhance the value and quality of family life, and to make sure that parents are supported in bringing up their children.

www.ncb.org.uk
National Children's Bureau (NCB)
Is a charity that offers information, advice, support and consultancy services on children's needs to its members.

www.familylearningnetwork.com
The National Family Learning Network
Aims to provide free information and support to family learning practitioners, to facilitate the sharing of good practice and to promote family learning regionally, nationally and internationally.

www.parentinguk.org
Parenting UK
Is a national umbrella organisation for parenting education and support.

Fathers and Men
www.fatherhoodinstitute.org
The Fatherhood Institute
Is seeking to change work so that fathers can be more available to care for their children. To change education so that boys are prepared for future caring roles. To change supports to family life so that the caring role of fathers and father-figures is recognised and strongly supported.

www.uk.mkp.org
The Mankind Project of the United Kingdom
Provides a training programme for men called the New Warrior Training Adventure.

Freespace.virgin.net/stevey.b/Men4Change.htm
UK Men for Change Network
Is a national network of men who have agreed to act as local contact points for men looking for men's groups, or who are interested in menswork.

www.workingwithmen.org
Working with Men
Develops projects, initiatives and campaigns to benefit and support the development of boys, young men and adults.

The publishers accept no responsibility for any inaccuracies in the above information. The views expressed in the statements about the organisations are not necessarily those of the author.

215

INDEX

217